THE
YIN AND YANG
OF LEADERSHIP FOLLOWERSHIP

S. ART TERMORSHUIZEN

ECHO LIGHT, FLORIDA, U.S.A.

ISBN: 1-4392-5538-5
ISBN-13: 9781439255384
Library of Congress Control Number: 2009908707

DEDICATION

This book is dedicated to Adele the most superb yang to my every yin for over three decades already; thank you!

CONTENTS

INTRODUCTION

This manuscript breaks the leadership discussion into three parts including the essence of leadership, coaching as leadership communication, and finally, marriage as revealed by God in Scripture to illustrate the way even gender issues are rendered inconsequential by a healthy understanding of true leadership and responsible followership. Note carefully, most people constantly switch between these alternative roles daily! What is needed right upfront is a clear definition of how I define the term leadership and that is as follows- "leadership is that functional ability displayed in context as initiative in spite of lack of title or office, whereby others would be stimulated to follow." Followership is defined as- "acting upon the personal choice to follow leadership initiative with a positive response."

The eastern concept of the Yin and Yang[1] is employed in discussing the inherent dynamic dualistic tension between leadership and followership. This eastern philosophical concept proposes that two equal but opposite life forces exist,  which continually oppose each other to maintain equilibrium in life. If one dominates life gets out of balance and that is when bad things happen. I am strategically

1   http://www.wsu.edu/~dee/CHPHIL/YINYANG.HTM (accessed May 23, 2009).

employing the yin and yang concept of opposing forces in dynamic tension to illustrate the interplay between leadership and followership. I believe it is necessary to break away from the typical western model of social Darwinian leadership[2]– where life is reduced to survival of the fittest and by a process of natural elimination lesser beings lose out and the winner takes the spoilsemerging as the leader. This causes leaders to be perceived as winners–thereby reducing everyone else to 'followers' or the resultant social Darwinian status of loser. How else do we explain the current unbalanced obsession with leaders at the expense of followers? A dynamic tension is presumed to exist between the two equal but opposite forces of the yin and yang. Similarly, a healthy tension should exist between good leaders and their good followers, based on the essential role of each, for the dynamic to work effectively. It is a relationship of mutual dependence between the distinctive roles; each need to be well executed for success to be enjoyed by both. Good leadership therefore is worth little without equally good followership. Conversely, good followership is wasted on poor leadership. In this way I propose that leadership and followership in essence are merely functions responsibly assumed to achieve an agreed upon purpose. More significantly they often function independently of title and office norms. One should not therefore be viewed as positive and the other negative, anymore than either the yin or yang are superior. Both are needed for the dynamic to work effectively, mutually supporting and playing off each other to produce the best symbiotic result. Both are subject

2 *Richard Hofstadter & Eric Foner, Social Darwinism in American Thought (Boston, MA: Beacon Press, 1992).*

to negative connotations like: 'leaders are egotistical' and 'followers are dumb sheep'. These generalizations may each have historical merit, but will not solve the dilemma we face. I will make concrete proposals for a better way forward.

To start that journey forward it seems apparent communication needs vital upgrading between leaders and their followers. Coaching is therefore discussed as the superlative way for communication to be ramped up to a better level between leaders and followers but even more, between all employees. Coaching is revealed as the communication style most suitable to be implemented between mutually respectful people, but which can simultaneously be used as a significant tool for individual growth and enrichment as well. The nature of coaching communication is specifically what will be elaborated. Every organization and endeavor can be positively enhanced and made more productive by engaging the entire staff to communicate via coaching principles. Of course this will require an increased value being placed on followers by leaders, with a greater recognition of their essential function for company success. Up to this point nothing has been mentioned about the significant role gender plays in the workplace and how it impacts the leader follower-ship dynamic- it certainly can add to the tension. The final section we enter next seeks to address the gender aspect. This will be done by looking at what is revealed in Scripture about the mutual functioning of spouses within Christian marriage.

Finally then, the aforesaid components will be drawn together in an expose of how Christian marriage is ideally intended by God to model the leadership fol-lowership interplay as the dynamic tension between spouses, based on their appropriate communication. This relationship model will greatly impact their off-spring in such a home and they will then in turn be well prepared for appropriate communication in the real world themselves as healthy followers and emerg-ing on cue as functional leaders. This will establish the foundational model of leadership followership in society, where the typical organizational hierarchy of titles or salaries, will no longer blur the reality of the true leadership followership process. Gender issues will be ordered sensitively in accordance with what is found revealed about this in the Bible.

SECTION I - LEADERSHIP

CHAPTER I - THE ESSENCE OF LEADERSHIP

Leadership theory of the past few decades is seemingly trapped in the modern cultural milieu of pragmatism, and so consistently falls within that narrow gamut of thought. Usually the term leadership is being used in the organizational context of title and position. Whether one reads *Situational Leadership* by Paul Hersey[3] or *Servant Leadership* by Robert K. Greenleaf[4], with widely differing conclusions, the issue seems to focus on the manner and style of leading, rather than the concept of leading. So a host of pragmatic books have been written with the focus on the style of how 'to do' leadership with these indicators in some of their titles: *Primal Leadership*[5], *Fit to Lead*[6], *Empowered Leader*[7], *Values-Based Leadership*[8], *Leading the Revolution*[9] and even *Be a Leader for God' Sake*[10]. These are mostly discussions for people of title and position,

---

3   Paul Hersey, The Situational Leader (Escondido, CA: Center for Leadership Studies, Inc. 1984, 2004).
4   Robert K. Greenleaf, Servant Leadership (Mahwah, NJ: Paulist Press, 1977).
5   Daniel Goleman, Richard Boyatzis, Annie McKee, Primal Leadership (Boston, MA: Harvard School Press, 2002).
6   Christopher P. Neck, Tedd L. Mitchell, Charles C. Manz, Emmet C. Thompson II. Fit To Lead. (New York, NY: St Martin's Press, 2004).
7   Calvin Miller, The Empowered Leader. (Nashville, TN: Broadman & Holman Publishers, 1995).
8   Susan Smith Kuczmarski, Thomas D. Kuczmarski, Values Based Leadership. (Paramus, NJ: Prentice-Hall Inc., 1995).
9   Gary Hamel, Leading the Revolution (Boston MA: Harvard Business School Press, 2000).
10 Bruce Winston, Be a Leader for God's Sake (Virginia Beach, VA: School of Leadership Studies, 2002).

but of limited applicational value for those without. Robert Palestini[11] noted in his book:

> "What the literature on leadership fails to include, though, are the traits of an effective follower. After all, what good is a leader without followers? What is lacking, therefore, is a book on what characteristics and behaviors are manifested by good and effective followers. Because there are many more followers than there are leaders, it seems to me that a good number of individuals would find such insights invaluable."

It is therefore my intent to address leadership as a functional practice in communication. Leading at the most basic level is conscientiously doing what is required, in spite of what everyone else might be doing. Finding the motivation to do that consistently is at the heart of what I am suggesting, quite in spite of whether one wears the leader or follower label, in that precise moment. Permit me to illustrate from my experience to clarify my meaning. In a high school class shortly after racial integration in South Africa, a racist teacher- the leader is yet once again bullying a student of color in the class. All students are by definition followers and by their silence are tacitly approving the teacher's behavior. Should a student however choose to express personal objection to that bullying, they cease to follow and by their action provide alternate leadership to that of the teacher. Their behavior alone forces a fresh choice on every student to follow; only because lead-

---

11   Robert Palestini, *A PATH TO LEADERSHIP The Heroic Follower* (Lanham, MA: Rowman & Littlefield Education, 2006).

ership was manifest by one without title or office. This new leader by function is in grave danger of dire consequences. Is that leadership not therefore by definition of much more courageous and stellar substance? Yet by narrowly fixating on leadership by appointment alone, we risk missing a vast leadership reality before our eyes.

Why do we assume a title is required for these appropriate choices to be made, or why do we think granting a title will elevate performance? Leadership is therefore more realistically the way in which people wisely conduct themselves making appropriate choices which in turn influence the choices of others. Appointment to office with rank and privilege certainly endues that person with power. However, unless those designated to follow make the appropriate choice to do so, that power will not be able to be implemented as intended. In the heart of every individual choices are constantly being made. We do the bulk of the workforce- the followers, no favors by suggesting it is only the leaders who make choices. What is more, we do those leaders even less favor. The question is why are you deciding as you do?

We all get out of bed and start every new day with an attitude. What that attitude is, largely determines the way our day will go. That attitude is not related to title or position, as directly as title or position results from our attitude, all other factors being equal of course. As we proceed through our day stresses batter us from every which way and will change our attitude if we are not careful. What keeps our attitude positive and committed to appropriate choices? More importantly is there a fundamental difference between this process for leaders and followers? Not likely. If it can be shown that being human is far more significant than status or power, communication can be improved to bridge the current divide between leaders and followers, to the mutual benefit of both; with positive impact on the ever precious 'bottom line'. My call is for us to embrace the dualistic tension of the yin and yang as a conceptual model for exploring the dynamic tension between these equal but opposite leadership followership functions, intended for symbiotic success for the whole. If we can break away from our current fixation with the importance of leaders and grasp their impoverished existence, without the empowered workforce co-operating enthusiastically, we will have made good progress.

While reading many recent leadership books it has become increasingly hard to believe; not everybody wants the corner office with the view and six figure income plus benefits. It seems to be an unquestioned given that anyone with self-respect wants to be a leader. Is that fair or realistic? Is it possible that we are offending a great many self respecting followers who just want to do a good job and feel proud about their accomplishments? Abraham Maslow is culturally accepted as accurately explaining the hierarchical way people experience their personal needs. When we accept this concept just as he simply intended, and do not take it as prescriptive in any way, we learn that people are at different places in experiencing their needs and therefore very different in what motivates their immediate lifestyle. Some are barely surviving, while others are working on ultimate meaning and purpose issues. Can these again be separated into leader issues, or follower?

I hardly think so. The common factors that exist among all people though are a desire for respect, for recognition, for acceptance and for opportunity to perform. These are not necessarily even part of a hierarchy of needs, but more basic elements of the human condition. When grasped as so basic and fundamental, then people naturally act accordingly. When they are clearly following their approach with due diligence, it will be in spite of being called either leaders or followers. People lead when they take ownership and responsibility to make life work. When they do so among people, their choices influence them as leadership. This may well take place without any conscious awareness or intention.

When I dropped out of a difficult training program back in the eighties, another quiet and calm student friend of mine became very agitated with me and demanded that I go over to his home after College ended that day. Once there he and his wife proceeded to tear me apart for 'quitting'. The bottom line was they were 'riding in my shadow'; deriving their strength off my energy and could not fathom how he would graduate if I left. It was very real to them and yet I was oblivious to any such thing even existing! I was leading them through by just being myself as an individual student, without intentionally offering anything. It sure taught me to be more aware of influence I was exercising quite unintentionally, in this case as a simple follower I had emerged in their eyes as a leader.

In that simply way every follower can manifest the function of leadership and when in turn leaders are influenced by the example of followers, they are personally manifesting the function of followers at that point.

Leaders and followers are no longer pejorative terms when looked at this way. When outstanding individual followers among otherwise anonymous thousands in a production line, are personally at peace and motivated in their own skin, they stand out as leaders among those; merely going through the motions while feeling unappreciated and irrelevant. Leadership and followership in essence therefore boils down to personal attitude and resultant function. Likewise, are Chief Executive Officers not followers when being instructed by their boards? Or when on the shop floor, they are instructed by a floor steward? If we focus on function at that point, their titles no longer obscure their need to be followers, without however the slightest diminishing of their grandiose title and status.

Is the normal social Darwinian concept of the 'leader as winner', a helpful one, given the impact of the resulting title of 'loser' on all the rest? If we can see people as valuable for their unique contribution and celebrate that within the functional processes of their employment, we empower everyone to lead from where they are. Every person alive is an attitude shaper by the way we respect and honor people; giving them dignity they will embrace and perform significantly better. This is again equally true of both leaders and followers. Was President Bush an empowered leader after 9/11? How about when his popularity ratings plummeted during his second term? It seems he clearly led better with positive support, than he did with massive rejection and opposition. Was he leading or following during the latter period? Functionally, even his title and office did not prevent him from being perceived as a weak follower in his last years, instead of a powerful leader.

The more typical numerical situation though is for the billions of workers without any office or title, destined to be labeled followers. A negative connotation is associated with the word; so why not be honest and just say 'dumb sheep'? Nobody wants to be made to feel like a loser, let alone all the time by positional inferiority in a typical hierarchical system, hence the global trend away from the hierarchical style of leadership. However, helping people grasp the significance of their role in the organizational system makes what they do, a meaningful contribution, which in turn inspires them to take ownership of their position. Doing this as effectively as Ricardo Semler[12] does in his business down in Brazil, proves the value of his affirming approach to people, by his companies having the lowest employee turnover rate in his entire populous nation. People want to work where they will be acknowledged and regarded as having intrinsic worth, in spite of even a relatively lowly purpose in the company structure. People are also for the same basic reason, always on waiting lists applying to get into his companies.

The analogy of ballroom dancing aptly comes to mind when thinking about the dynamic tension inherent in the yin and yang of leadership and followership. Two people are in control of their own choices and resultant moves, with gender expectations in dancing demanding specific roles for each. The tension of the dynamic dualism is set into motion. The man proposes

---

12 Ricardo Semler, *The Seven Day Weekend* (New York, NY: Portfolio, 2004).

a direction by his movement, as he seeks to lead his partner. As she trusts him, she in turn chooses to follow his lead and flows smoothly after his movement. If his proposal is met by her trusting response, those two choices blend harmoniously into a beautiful dance of balanced tensions from their opposing roles. People watching will never remark about an individual in such a dance as being beautifully gifted and a superb dancer. The entire beauty is in the symbiotic production of two combining into one smooth movement, in harmonious interpretation of the music. If in this case the man fails to lead, or conversely the woman fails to respond with trust and follow, no beautiful dance can be produced. Both are equally crucial to the process of finding balance between their separate functions, and no fair-minded person can legitimately state the leadership is more vital or valid- than the responsive following. Certainly the case can be made for the leader needing to take the initiative to get the process going, but that subtle necessity calls forth a different function between two equals, hardly a superior role.

My desire is to apply enough emphasis on the role of the follower to bring the discussion of leadership back into a reasonably realistic balance. Currently leaders are discussed as almost operating in a vacuum, the followers seem so peripheral to the whole enterprise. Can a leader function alone? No, because without followers they are not a leader, but merely a successful individual. By definition a leader needs followers. Is it possible for those followers however, to complete an assignment successfully, by mutual cooperation without any visible individual leader? Certainly! So while leaders need followers, followers do not equally need leaders. However, some unifying goal or assignment is needed at a minimum. This is why I am convinced leadership emerges spontaneously among capable followers as the need arises, making leadership largely a function of attitude and gifting in context. When people are empowered to flow in their gifting and passion, on a team for an agreed upon organizational purpose, the scenario is in place for amazing things to happen. The bottom line will happen and people will grow, while loving their work; who mentioned anything about titles or power over them?

CHAPTER II - THE GLOBAL CHALLENGE

Culture has a sobering way of correcting us when we think our titles are of much importance. As the world increasingly becomes a functional global village it is important for us to allow these cultural sensitivities to broaden our outlook to how leadership actually functions in spite of titles.

South Africa is officially led by an elected President. Decades ago Nelson Mandela was not officially a leader in South Africa; to the government he was a common terrorist, lucky enough to spend decades in jail and not pay for treason with his life. Here we have a classic case of a follower who refused to do so and eventually nearly brought the country to a standstill. He was simply a man of courage who refused to let the system deprive him of an inalienable right he sensed within. That personal vision caused him to be a follower of a higher cause, than the mere racist political machine which could only imprison his body. By the end of the twentieth century, he became the premier leader of hope and symbol of prevailing justice in the world. During those thirty plus years, dating from his trial in 1961, who was really leading in South Africa? The masses had been silenced for so long because no Mandela had emerged before; without office or election, and just their confidence in him alone to 'unofficially' lead them. This could so easily have gone other ways and ended disastrously.

Often those who lead mass people movements begin without title or office, but quickly claim those and then move on to perform ghastly atrocities under that cover of 'official sanction'. Mandela[13] showed uncommon humility and when he received his title, wore it lightly for a brief season before relinquishing it again.

Why Mandela? Among the forty million other suffering black people, did no others arise as followers of a higher cause? Certainly many did, empowered by the courage of Mandela. Steve Biko was one of the brighter lights to shine; a follower who was comfortable in his own skin even when that deeply offended the powers with authority. He could easily be likened in intellect and rhetorical power to the American 'Malcolm X'. Why did he not make an international impact like Mandela? He was not in prison as a global figure of liberation like Mandela, and police were able to kill him without any official consequences to the guilty parties. The point is people can die while following and we afford followers no just respect by failing to understand the cost not to be a mellow sheep, even when millions around them are choosing to do so. You may legitimately question why Steve Biko is called a follower here and not a leader, because that is precisely my point. If we use the term leader as one having a title and holding an office, Steve Biko was just another nobody; he was not an official leader of anyone, or anything. However, his courage and personal convictions as Bantu Steve Biko rattled the entire regime into bloodthirsty action to have him permanently silenced.

---

13   Nelson Mandela, Long Walk to Freedom (London: Abacus, 1994).

Many of the most powerful people of the current global scene are not so, due to title or office either. Warren Buffet the most influential investor the world has ever seen; who personally turned thirty plus of his best friends into multi millionaires through the mere power of suggestion, holds no office outside his self-built company. Richard Branson began as a teenager and likewise without title or office, built VIRGIN into a billion dollar global empire of vast influence based in England. Britain itself is an interesting anomaly in the discussion of titles and leadership. Annually the queen ceremoniously uses her power to elevate 'commoners'- those without title or inherent status in society, who have had uncommon success, to the elite status of Lord and Ladies. Alex Ferguson became Sir Alex Ferguson by building a soccer empire at Manchester United, while Richard Branson became Sir Richard Branson, to name but two such fairly recent cases. Did those titles in any way impact their success or cause it? Absolutely not! The exercise the queen performs is merely a cultural need the British apparently still have to keep their society based on class differentiation, while most of the rest of the world moves quite uniformly and strongly to diminish class differences. Leadership in this new world is clearly based on more substantial things than titles and corresponding offices.

CHAPTER III - FORM VS FUNCTION

Robert Palestini[14] speaks about practice being based on sound theory to be able to work effectively. When practice fails it is time to return to the basics and that is the business concept of 'function preceding form'. It seems this is precisely what is currently needed for the church. Church leadership requires a highly specific form of leadership. Tragically what normally happens, regardless of the theological system in place, is usually a man is employed with a title and expected to lead the congregation. What is specifically then done to allow room for Jesus to be the Head of the church- His body, which He still claims to be? Rarely much, if anything at all! It is no small wonder therefore the church is in the advanced state of decay it finds itself in, when compared to the model and intent for it revealed in Scripture. For substantiation of this bold claim any number of very up to date studies is available; try Barna and Viola[15]- Pagan Christianity just for starters. Practice as Palestini spoke of it, plainly does not work in this case, yet a huge reluctance exists to return to the theory and see where we went so wrong.

Titles for church leaders like pastor, preacher, padre, vicar and so forth, are all extra biblical and find no

14 Robert Palestini, A Path To Leadership The Heroic Follower (Lanham, MA: Rowman & Littlefield Education, 2006).
15 Frank Viola & George Barna, Pagan Christianity (Carol Stream, IL: Tyndale House Publishers, Inc., 2008).

precedent in Scripture- 'the theory', for appointing offices in the local church. Talk about denominational 'corporate' offices is equally beyond the revealed Word of God and clearly these exist to the detriment of God's intent, exclusively in manmade religion. Why for instance do most churches have 'boards' running them, when nothing of the sort is ever mentioned in Scripture? Since God did not reveal them and faith only comes from what is revealed (Romans 10:17), they can by definition, never be of faith. Yet without faith it is impossible to please God (Hebrews 11:6a). But the entire reason for the church's existence is to please God! We certainly did not receive freedom from God to make form fit function, as we please, especially when it resists His intention.

Ephesians lists ministry gifts which God has blessed the local expression of the body with, to grow it in the way He intends (4:11-13). These ministry gifts are people functioning in ways the body needs. Four or five such gifts are mentioned depending on the way the text is read. Rarely however do any of these ministries make it into local church leadership titles, because one has come to exclusively dominate the entire church scene- pastor. This has been happening erroneously for so long now it seems quite improper to challenge the notion. But while discussing leadership it is imperative to leave no stone unturned, sacred or not, if one intends to arrive at Truth. The entire concept of pastors running local churches, which they often offensively refer in turn to as 'my church', cannot be extrapolated from Scripture into any form of Truth.

Since God firstly calls local churches to be run by a group of elders (Presbyterian government) and not by any individual gift ministry, the onus is upon those claiming to believe the revelation of God's Word, to substantiate why they function differently to what it clearly reveals (James 5:14, 1 Peter 5:1). Three words function synonymously in Scripture- bishop, overseer and elder. These are always and only shown in Scripture to be functioning plurally in singular locations. Since Jesus is the only head of the church wherever it manifests, even the term elder is not meant as a title, but purely as a function, although from Scripture it can be an office from which to serve the people. Is it not crystal clear how damaging this church situation is when we discuss leadership and followership? Where is the dynamic dualism of the yin and yang holding out hope of a symbiotic solution, when the pastor is the ruler and the rest mere followers? Sure he can use his gifts but what do the rest of the body do with theirs, while he controls the entire show? Followership by the church masses needs to be seriously revisited if the church is ever to become the bride of Christ; spotless and without blemish[16].

16 *Ephesians 5:27*

CHAPTER IV - FOLLOWERSHIP OPTIONS

Eventually, although still in a hopeless minority, some leadership books are now also being written on followership issues. S.S. Seteroff[17] says: "It has become apparent to me that we cannot address leadership without examining followership. True followership is the result of achieving the capacity to be a leader, and not before." He is grappling with the same idea I am, that followers emerge as leaders by the way they function. I could call them 'mature' followers, to differentiate from other generic followers, but avoid doing so because of the issue surrounding definition of terms. While Friedman[18] continues the concept by making the case for less hierarchical organizations based on globalization as follows: "By in large, it is the increase in risk and the globalization that brings such rapid and radical change as to increase the need for flatter and more responsive organizations." Organizations that is, in which followers will be elevated in status and empowered to become increasingly effective contributors to the bottom line. Organizations in which, by definition leaders will be less overbearing and powerful. Margaret Wheatley[19] weighed in on the dynamic dualism of the

---

17 Sviatoslav Steve Seteroff, Beyond Leadership to Followership (Victoria, BC: Trafford Publishing, 2003).

18 T. L. Friedman, The Lexus and the Olive Tree (New York: Farrar Straus Giroux. 1999).

19 M. J. Wheatley, Leadership and the New Science: Discovering Order in a Chaotic World (San Francisco: Berrett-Koehler, 1999).

leadership followership tension with the valuable insight that on high performance teams situational leaders would emerge from among the followers as the need arose, giving credence to her conviction that organizations are 'leader full'. Precisely my conviction that the leadership function will emerge in context, by inspired followers owning the task and excelling in their empowerment.

Barbara Kellerman[20] of Harvard has weighed in substantially on followership with her latest book:

> "This book on followers deliberately departs from the leadercentric approach that dominates our thinking about how power, authority, and influence are exercised. It claims that to obsess about superiors at the expense of subordinates is to distort the dynamic between them. And it sends a message: to underestimate, or to undervalue, the importance of those whom Shakespeare once referred to as underlings is to disempower them. So long as we fixate on leaders at the expense of followers, we will perpetuate the myth that they don't much matter."

It would be hard to read her compelling book and not be converted to this better way of seeing organizations moving forward realistically. She also enumerated on the idea that effective 'whistle blowers' have ceased to be mere followers, but by their actions morphed into leaders. My words would be that they have contextually functioned as leaders at that point, in spite of

---

20   Barbara Kellerman, *Followership: how followers are creating change and changing leaders* (Boston, MA: Harvard Business School Publishing, 2008).

their status as followers. Her book was written in the leadership mold but is most definitely for everyone's enlightenment:

> "First, as we know from our own experience, the line that separates superiors from their subordinates is often blurred. Sometimes leaders and managers follow; and sometimes followers lead. In addition, the line between them tends to shift. Some of us are followers most of the time and leaders some of the time. Others are the opposite: leaders most of the time and followers some of the time. Finally, many of us are superiors and subordinates simultaneously."

While these truisms are already written up, my contribution is along the lines of an altogether other dimension of following. My next quote from Kellerman sets the stage for my disclosure by her saying, "We are followers first in infancy and childhood of the adults on whom we depend, and then later in life we follow leaders before we lead followers."

All true believers in Jesus should be following Him as their supreme priority regardless of our age or any other criteria. Then these following characteristics will be present by virtue of the fruit of the indwelling Holy Spirit in their lives found in Galatians 5: "[22]But the fruit of the Spirit is love, joy, peace, patience, kindness, goodness, faithfulness, [23]gentleness, self-control; against such things there is no law."[21] So if these believers who are firstly followers are called to function as leaders, they are also in possession of the aforementioned

---

21 Bible (Nashville, TN: Broadman, 1999).

general characteristics and should therefore usually make superior leaders. Is this not what Jesus intended when He called all people to follow Him and only then reach out to lead the entire world into the same followership? So once again my conviction, when discussing the essence of leadership, is that all people are meant to be followers, and His followers are meant to lead, as appointed by God, when the appropriate situation arrives and not wait to also be anointed or appointed by men.

That supreme calling should alone adequately empower leadership under most circumstances. Every believer has the duty to lead others to Christ. Sure this expectation is an anomaly to ordinary earthly life and is a serious departure from its leadership norms, but is it actually incorrect, or is life incorrect, in demanding only official leaders may function with leadership? No leader can accurately or honestly claim they were called to lead anything as a higher priority, than they were called to follow Christ. Hence followership by essence always precedes everything else, including emerging as a leader. Leadership is also generally accepted to be the role of the more mature and yet not so with followership of Jesus. Jesus calls us all to emulate little children as we follow Him. Would leadership not be a more mature and godly experience for all, if leaders were all required to be apprenticed to Jesus as followers, before taking any official title or office as a leader?

The study of the essence of leadership has brought me to the place of understanding the quality of leadership corresponding to the quality of individual followership of Jesus as that leader's Lord. Until we leave our individual all on the altar in sacrifice to Him, one is not yet ready to assume leadership worthy of His Name. The strongest leader then is as weak as their service before the Lord as His follower. This ought to help leaders better appreciate the symbiotic nature of the yin and yang dynamic dualistic relationship between following and leading. Not that this is a new idea; James Nolan[22] already functioned off his basic premise in 1984, that leadership and followership were of equal importance. I am merely tightening the definition of a follower to following Jesus at His open invitation, as of first importance.

As a contrast to this pure expectation, Malagant is the epitome of a failed follower in the film First Knight[23], when he leads a rebellion against the overtly Christian rule of King Arthur. Having been the first knight himself and tiring of the humble servant nature of the king, he tries to overthrow the king and usurp power. His leadership style is brutal and tyrannical. Machiavelli[24] would be proud of his justification of right made by might. This leadership style of his, knows no following and claims independence of thought, yet is as old as the rebellion of Lucifer himself; tiring of following, he too desired to lead (Isaiah 14:12-20). What is therefore equally unsurprising is that he should also do so with his motivation of pride.

Why then, believers strive for leadership when God primarily calls us to followership, is not equally clear. How

22 J. S. Nolan, Followership Greater Than or Equal to Leadership (Education, 104(3), 311-312, 1984).
23 Jerry Zucker, Director- First Knight, (1995).
24 Nicolo Machiavelli, The Prince (1505).

often is leadership manifested without title or office to provide official recognition? Is it not then appropriate to assume people want power and privilege now for instant gratification, more than the satisfaction of hearing 'well done good and faithful servant' later from the Master? That is more pragmatically satisfying than a long-term hope of a future; but yet unseen reward.

The essence of leadership can be more clearly seen when leadership becomes a function of following Christ through faith obedience and doing what is needed at the right time, regardless of title or office. Followers of Christ in that way manifest more leadership than all the titles and offices available across the globe daily. Since obedience to Him is the highest human calling, then followership holds more dignity than any office or title this world can offer.

This is in no way an attempt to nullify leadership by office or title. Rather the essence of leadership has been shown to be complete without these earthly accruements, but not necessarily discounted by them. Wonderful people of both genders and many cultures have taken offices with titles and shown remarkable leadership ability; too many to mention here with any satisfaction indeed. However, a subtle undertone to this search for the essence of leadership has revealed that often great leaders lack the passion for either title or office. They are usually inspired; either by God or at least by a vision, and making a significant difference is usually their biggest motivator. Gandhi wanted to see his land freed from colonial rule. Mandela wanted to see all people free to grow and develop without the limitations of racism excluding the masses. Jesus wanted to deliver people from slavery; to religion and the bondages of darkness and ignorance, resulting from sin.

If Jesus is God, and the biggest single religions in the world's followers say the Bible is correct in saying He is, then surely we would be remiss to ignore what He as deity, invited humans to do. He said "Come follow Me!" Nobody can do better than to obey God. A comprehensive study of the entire Bible can find no similar command to 'Lead'. The priority sequence has thus been established for people by revelation; first we follow Jesus and then we will lead as the situational context requires.

Scripture does commend those who seek to lead as service to their Lord (1 Timothy 3:1). However, what is far more typical is that God uses those who are already active and serving followers of Jesus to do more specific things at His bidding. All through Scripture we see people being led into more strategic functions for God's purposes to be accomplished. If these people were not following God in the first place, He would not have been able to steer them more specifically into new avenues. God does not seem to be impressed with those on their own mission for Him. Rather He likes to use those obedient to His call and available to obey His instructions. A healthy church is always one where He can gloriously be the Head, in the leading role with everyone else merely the supporting cast, without their own glory.

Following God is the highest call any person can achieve in this life. No leadership position will ever achieve the glory God intends for those who follow obediently by faith. History shows the greatest positive impacts on humanity have been made by obedient people God then used to lead in directions of His choosing. Noah saved humanity when God chose to judge all evil by a global flood. Noah was neither a boat builder, nor near any water and did not even comprehend the concept of rain because it had never happened before. Yet he obeyed God and human life was successfully preserved on earth. Joseph was also not a leader, but a slave following God when he emerged into leadership. Moses followed God and led God's people out of bondage in Egypt, but clearly not because he firstly was some great leader. The case can be strongly made for his being a great follower of God first though. Saul on the other hand was the people's choice as leader and yet with leadership aptitude, but without following God, he was a dismal failure. The history of Israel reveals leaders could be great by virtue of impact by following God, or similarly great while being evil and corrupt, but never good while being the latter. So it seems leadership is certainly possible without following God, but the goodness and positive impact of that leadership, will never approach or rival the impact of primarily first following God.

CHAPTER V - CHARACTER OF LEADERS

Looking as I have been at the essence of leadership, I now focus on the essentials agreed upon by many secular and sacred scholars. I emphasize the internal nature of their personal belief systems, mainly to show that a good deal of congruence exists among leadership expectations abroad, in spite of the radically different worldviews espoused by each party. However, since I am comparing and contrasting leadership with followership to show the dynamic dualism between these inseparable roles, no difference exists between the characteristics required of both. If leaders are simply more mature followers, then these characteristics apply to all equally. For clarification I define 'mature' as that composite quality of self confidence and humility, that chooses to seek the best for those around them before themselves.

Flexibility: appears repeatedly in research readings on the essence of leadership. An illustration from the Army situation follows:

> "Flexibility has become one of the many essential characteristics of a leader in today's Army, and this has been proven on the battlefields in Afghanistan and Iraq. One of the ways that we can help leaders become more adaptive to these changes is to incorporate more real-world

experiences into their training plans as well as at the various combat training centers."[25]

Adaptability is a synonym for what is required to prepare for all the change going on today. Robert Palestini[26] put it as follows"

> "W. Edwards Deming said that healthy organizations are ones that are continually improving. The same thing can be said of individuals. Continuous improvement assumes change. Therefore, if the heroic follower is to be effective, he or she must become an agent of change, or at the very least be tolerant of change. Thus, the habit of flexibility or adaptability is essential."

This, sounds like the often repeated and so called 'missing be-attitude' from the Sermon on the Mount by Jesus: "Blessed are the flexible, for they shall bend but never break."

Emotional Intelligence: Daniel Goleman's insights and the resulting exposure we now have about this area, certainly places it near the top of leadership requirements. Some naysayers claim, leadership cannot be discounted because EI is not very high in the individual and this seems true enough. However, that is because we have failed to adequately define the essence of leadership. Leaders may have been very effective even though not nice at all, like many dictators, many ED's / CEO's and people willing to be elevated to the

---

25 Joseph Claburn, "Flexibility: today's leaders adjust, adapt, overcome," (Infantry Magazine, March-April, 2004).
26 Robert Palestini, A Path To Leadership The Heroic Follower (Lanham, MA: Rowman & Littlefield Education, 2006).

highest rungs of power, without firstly being equipped with high EI. That does not detract from their ability to lead, but it certainly would detract those following. In the essence of leadership, one in possession of high EI is always to be favored to lead by followers. Nelson Mandela, Mahatma Gandhi and Jesus Christ, are but three global leaders who in spite of lack of title or office, in their own time evidenced amazing emotional intelligence. Each made an indelible impact largely because of their EI and how that alone drew followers to their cause. Even natural enemies to each were disarmed by their amazingly mature persona.

Motivation: this covers the reaction people have to who the leaders actually are as people. This is the major single dimension which garners followers for leaders. People want to follow the lead of a motivator. This is about much more than mere passion. Hitler for instance was a passionate speaker who was described as electrifying to his audiences. This statement was made by one of his close confidants, Leon Degrelle:[27] "His face showed emotion or indifference according to the passion or apathy of the moment. Even his complexion, otherwise dull, lit up as he spoke. And at such times, to be sure, Hitler was strangely attractive and as if possessed of magic powers." However that sweeping emotion is not necessarily motivational into real action. Effective leaders inspire a positive reaction in people to act, respond and serve. As Marquardt and Berger explain in their treatise, "Global Leaders for the Twenty First Century":

27 Leon Degrelle, *The Enigma of Hitler (The Journal for Historical Review, Volume 14 number 3, May/June 1994).*

"What is Carol Bartz's own concept of leadership? She describes it as "Motivating people to meet goals. Leaders help people believe in their goals and inspire them to deliver on their promises. Leaders instill a sense of purpose and urgency." Without motivation, you might just as well not be there"[28]

In this sense, leaders are those doing the bulk of influencing, inspiring, empowering and motivating, by virtue of who they are as people and how they function as a result.

Truthfulness: In spite of the popularity of Bill Clinton and his infamous strategy of creative deceit through ongoing lying; which proved very successful for him, the research shows that most people still rate truthfulness as a desired characteristic in leaders. Liars are hard to promote because they are not trusted and therefore undependable. Likewise, it is hard to follow someone who is inherently untrustworthy; how do you know where you are being led? This is a remarkable inconsistency in society at present, where lying seems to be very acceptable as the normal human condition. Yet as Charles Handy notes: "Tom Peters devotes a whole chapter in his book Liberation Management to "The Missing X-Factor: Trust," but has no easy solutions to offer. "Read more novels and fewer business books," he says. "Relationships really are all there is."[29] Yet, how do relationships of any consequence get de-

---

28 Michael J. Marquardt & Nancy O. Berger et al., *Global Leaders for the Twenty First Century (New York: State University of New York Press, 2000).*
29 Charles Handy, *The Age of Paradox (Boston: Harvard Business School Press, 1995).*

veloped without the foundational context of truth? Can believability really be dispensed with? Trust is unwise in a context of deceit, yet relationships need trust as a cardinal value to have any hope of building into anything of on-going significance. The term 'truthiness'; has even been coined to raise the believability of your own personal version of the reality. While the comedian Stephen Colbert[30] may have been making a joke with this term, everybody seems to have latched onto it as just what they were looking for, to keep on lying without feeling bad. Even the Dialect Society accepted the word as their top new word for 2005.

Humility: Contrary opinions exist as to the legitimacy of this characteristic and they divide for the most part quite clearly between believers and those of secular persuasion. Clearly being of the former persuasion myself, I offer the positive appreciation for this essential character trait. Marilyn K. Lustgarten put it this way:

> "Humility, which is the acknowledgment of the truth about who we are in relationship to others, is absolutely essential to effective leadership. G.K. Chesterton once said, "It is always the secure who are humble." A leader secure enough to admit that he or she doesn't have, or need to have, all the answers is rewarded with the contributions of talented followers committed to the success of the whole organization. Jim Collin's research, which became the basis for his watershed book "Good to Great," is full of examples

30 Merriam-Webster, *review of The Colbert Report*, by Stone Phillips (Stephen Colbert, ColbertNation.com), October 17, 2005.

of organizations that have consistently outper-formed their peers over time when led by an in-dividual with the paradoxical qualities of deep personal humility and unwavering perseverance towards stated goals."[31]

We have just celebrated the birthday of Abe Lincoln for the two hundredth time and this man still stands as one of the great men of humility in American life. 'Honest Abe' is what he has been known as. All leaders would do well to follow his strategy of honest deference to others, in spite of tremendous personal gifting and con-tributions made. His respect for his fellow human be-ings was what he communicated and feeling respected affects the way people respond and perform. This is the quiet confident dimension of all valued leadership.

Courage/Integrity: Followers of Jesus Christ are duty bound to their Creator to use their brains effectively. But knowing this, leaders are also meant to inspire fol-lowers and that takes courage. If one realizes it is often a thankless role, but still a role which needs to be ful-filled and one is willing to do so regardless, takes cour-age. It has been famously said that courage, is not the absence of fear, but action with or despite fear. Titles and Offices often put a 'target on the leader's back' and 'heavy lies the head which wears the crown'. Leader-ship is not for those who want an easy passage. Few things make leadership look feeble without major sin, like the lack of courage rapidly does. Another dimen-sion of this is the authentic courage of integrity. People

31   Marilyn Lustgarten,""Humility - A Leadership Imperative," Ezine @rticles, April 7, 2008, http://ezinearticles.com/?Humility—A-Leadership-Imperative&id=1094341/ (accessed March 28, 2009).

who lead are significantly more responsible to manifest congruence between their walk and talk. "Felipe Alfonso sees integrity as one of the most important qualities of a good leader. It is not just honesty," he says, "but that I am who I am wherever I go."[32] What comes from their mouth must be backed up all the way by what they do and how they act.

Observation: is that characteristic curiosity which is typical of most excellent leaders and therefore forms part of the essence of a leader. This ability to notice and perceive more than most actually observe, is what gives them their 'bright eyes'. As the authors Sue Mackey & Laura Tonkin, put it in '*Living Well, Working Smart*'- "Much of what we learn in life results directly from our ability to observe. There is a wealth of knowledge to be gained by observing people and the world around us. That wealth of knowledge is gained via our ability to observe with a purpose – to learn and to understand. Although each of us possesses the capacity to observe, highly successful people do it constantly."[33] Leaders see more than most because they are looking critically and interpreting constantly as they see. In the popular British investigation series Sherlock Holmes, he and Dr Watson are camping out, when he awakes and asks Dr Watson what he observes. Challenged Dr Watson draws on his deepest powers and regales Sherlock Holmes about the stars and galaxies overhead. To which Sherlock simply answers; "Our tent is gone." Leaders have the uncanny ability to observe

---

32 Michael J Marquardt & Nancy O. Berger et al., Global Leadership for the Twentieth Century (New York: State University of New York Press, 2000).
33 Sue Mackey & Laura Tonkin et al., Living Well, Working Smart (Bothwell, WA: The Mackey Group Publishers Network, 2005).

and then separate information by appropriate value and relevance.

Faith: this is explained in secular leadership studies, very differently to the way the Bible defines it. However, a believer would have it both ways, if they are truly a believer as the Bible describes. The secular faith in a leader is defined as that quality of belief inspired in the team and what they are doing; an expectation of what they will be able to achieve. For a believer, it adds the dimension of also hearing the Word of the Lord and walking in obedience to it. Romans 10:17 'So faith comes from hearing, and hearing by the word of Christ.'[34] Faith ought to raise the optimism of leaders in the face of all challenges and inspire the team of followers to come through victoriously in the heat of the battle. When the followers are filled with faith they in turn carry the leader along with them, proving the symbiotic nature of collective faith. Many amazing stories are told in the Bible about leaders obeying God even when the requirement seemed ridiculous and with the followers all obeying, amazing feats were performed. Joshua did not use a strategy to conquer Jericho as much as he used faith to obey God's instructions. Admittedly those instructions seemed absurd. Yet the city was taken according to the predicted schedule. Faith enabled Joshua to carry on in spite of looking foolish and in due time God vindicated that faith obedience.

Providing a summary for this section on the character of leaders and followers I am using what Chip Bell stated as follows:

34 *Bible (Nashville: Broadman, 1999).*

"Great leaders are confident enough to show *humility*. And humility promotes a partnering relationship rather than a parenting relationship. Great leaders create *emotional safety* through the *courage* and the attentive *curiosity* they foster IN others. Great leaders are generous with their *advice* (given in a fashion that does not surface resistance), their *feedback* (delivered in a manner that does not unearth resentment), their *stories* (told in a way that stirs passion as well as sparks insight), their *support* (provided to ensure their associates have backing and assistance), and their *focus* (given to ensure associates have a sense of direction, purpose, and vision). Now, look back on all the words in italics and you will discover the human architecture of today's leader. The way of the mentor is the way of the leader, particularly in today's brain-based economy."[35]

I appreciate this concise summary, but beg to differ slightly on the mentor bit; in that the way of a leader today is preferably the way of a coach and much more of that in the next section. What we have seen then is that leadership and followership are involved in a symbiotic relationship when it works properly. One is not a superior nor the other an inferior role or status. Both are required to fulfill a function. These two roles are in a dynamic tension of opposite functions. All leaders are also followers in specific situations and many followers also lead, but title and offices have less to do with

---

35 Chip R. Bell, *Managers as Mentors: Building Partnerships for Learning* (San Francisco: Berrett-Koehler Publishers, Inc., 2002).

this than functioning in context; according to skills and abilities. What is crucial therefore, is that leaders communicate with followers in such a manner that followership is inspired in them. In the next section I want to address that communication specifically through what coaching has to offer.

SECTION II - COACHING

CHAPTER VI - THE ESSENCE OF COACHING

The first section closed with a summary of characteristics aptly describing great leaders. However, it was also seen that since the dynamic dualism exists between leadership and followership, those characteristics would apply equally well to great followers. By definition then, a follower is not a wannabe leader, but a person responsibly functioning in the context of their position to the faithful best of their abilities. By doing so they will automatically be leading since that is what the very nature of those characteristics implemented mean. I trust the yin and yang metaphor is becoming clearer to your thinking processes, as we see more clearly how we cannot have one without the other and they are definitely in constant tension. That emphasizes how urgently we need to unbundle the confusion surrounding the great man leader theory, still all too common today. Is that not what we expect the US president to be? Yet without many competent people actually implementing the plans he will get nothing done. Seeing the inevitable tension between these two inseparable opposites in leadership followership, we must make every effort to improve understanding and communication. Hopefully that will lead directly to increased mutual respect, and that desire is what steers us into this section on coaching.

The most recent addition to the soft sciences over the past twenty years has been the newly expanded and defined role of coaching. Previously only the sports coach was in view, but today coaching has many facets. Daniel Harkavy clarifies:

> "Coaching is not management consulting. It is not psychological counseling. It's not personal training. It is nothing short of a new way to think about managing and leading and living with and for others. It is as practical and tangible as it is conceptual and comprehensive. Effective leadership is all about taking followers on a journey that enables them to experience and accomplish more as a result of the coaching and vision you bring to them. Great leaders take special and obvious delight in developing their people. That's the crucial difference."[36]

The crucial difference that is, between mere leaders and great ones. What I am trying to show is the dynamic tension between leading and following as two parts of the same issue. Therefore, to talk about coaching empowering leaders is also to talk about coaching to empower followers. Coaching is not intended to perpetuate the unhealthy emphasis on leaders at the peril of followers. Here, coaching is being offered as the communication style to further level the entire playing field for all. Sviatoslav Steve Seteroff[37] put it this way, "We must recognize that while we may head an

---

36 Daniel Harkavy, *Becoming a Coaching Leader* (Nashville, TN: Thomas Nelson, Inc., 2007).
37 Sviatoslav Steve Seteroff, *Beyond Leadership to Followership* (Victoria, BC: Trafford Publishing, 2003).

organization, a portion of it, or are responsible for a process, we are merely stewards of the assets we are charged with, and our people are human capital to also be conserved and encouraged." Do leaders expect to be served by the people or to serve the people themselves? Increasingly I sense the latter is proving true. Coaching is a way to leverage the company's most vital asset for all they are worth.

Coachville.com[38] is currently the largest network of coaches with over 10,000 members, and I like what they explain about the whole field of coaching:

> "We've found that coaching is so powerful because of the "who" element. Goals (what) and strategies (how) are terrific, but unless they are integrated with the person (who), they will take longer to accomplish, probably not be what the person really wants, and not result in the high levels of happiness and fulfillment that are possible. The client and coach can start at any of the three portals (who, what, or how), and weave through all three, as needed, during the coaching process."

The authors of *Co-Active Coaching*[39] express their enthusiasm for coaching this way: "In today's world, coaching is both a growing profession worldwide and a growing communication style adopted by leaders in organizations, teachers, counselors, parents, and

---

38 *CoachVille.com, The Coaching Starter Kit: Everything You Need to Know to launch and Expand Your Coaching Practice (New York, NY: W. W. Norton & Company, Inc., 2003).*

39 *Laura Whitworth et al., Co-Active Coaching (2nd ed.) (Mountain View, CA: Davies-Black Publishing, 2007).*

others." While I readily acknowledge coaching is far more than just the one narrow dimension of communication selected for this focus, I postulate that it is precisely this dimension which causes it to grow so vigorously. Coaching is creating a self perpetuating momentum by the affirming approach which enables better communication between people; especially those spending large amounts of time together by virtue of work or being married. An example illustrates the power of coaching over a brief six month period in Jeff's life where 360 degree feedback reviews before and after, revealed the need to work on and the resultant outcome of the coaching intervention:

> "Jeff is a senior executive and passionate leader with a strong track record and radically ambitious business goals. However, passion translated into an overbearing style that sometimes left team members out in the cold. Jeff knew he had to change his own behavior in order to build the level of teamwork that his challenging goals required. A 360 review exercise provided telling feedback on how his style was impeding progress.
>
> A follow-up 360 review six months later provided solid evidence that Jeff was listening better, and effectively eliciting input from others. The group is on track toward their goal."[40]

Communication and relationships can usually both be improved and coaching is a significant help to that end.

---

40 http://www.dougsilsbee.com/coaching/cases accessed June 11, 2009.

John Whitmore[41] confidently stated his expectation in his 2002 treatise:

> "Only when coaching principles govern, or underlie all management behavior and interactions, as they certainly will do in time, will the full force of people's performance potential be released." He continued to elaborate why-: "coaching delivers results in large measure because of the supportive relationship between the coach and the coachee, and the means and style of communication used."

It is imperative to acknowledge the context into which coaching has burst forth as a solution. Communication is always problematic in organizations and human relationships and something that needs to be worked hard on by most to achieve success. However, many are not working on it simply because they fail to realize how extensive this problem really is. Many simply do not realize they are going about communication in an unhelpful way. Like the overtly honest person who constantly feels the need to vocally express all they are sensing, for truth to prevail. That is not generally considered helpful.

But what about the communication sent to workers when certain followers are elevated, by title and office into the realm of the superior- leaders, while everyone not likewise promoted, is by the same action then relegated to what must become known as the ranks of the inferior- followers. The accruements of title, like special

41   John Whitmore, *Coaching For Performance (Boston, MA: Nicholas Brealey Publishing, 2002).*

parking bays, offices and access, all contribute to an unseen but tangible divider, running through the organization. How can the masses feel wanted, accepted or approved in that divisive organizational climate? Ferdinand Fournies[42] has some strong words for the current confusion between leaders (managers) and followers as separate species. Speaking to managers he said:

> "Because people around you do what you tell them, you become even more impressed with your own importance. But what has happened is that you have become deluded into believing that you are the most important member of that group. Because you believe they need you more than you need them, you treat them accordingly. You get involved in self-destructive behavior. You stop managing; you just keep score. The sad but true fact is that you need them more than they need you. You can't get the job done without them."

Only about 45% of workers[43] in the US claimed to be satisfied with their jobs. Work is therefore, at least for more than half of adult workers, something to be done and then fled as soon as possible. The current depressed economic state has somewhat changed this by making those with employment at least grateful for the most part to have it. What does coaching offer this situation? John Whitmore adds his conviction as follows:

---

42 Ferdinand F. Fournies, Coaching for Improved Work Performance, (New York, N.Y.: McGraw Hill Professional Publishing, 2000).
43 http://www.careervision.org/About/PDFs/MR_JobSatisfaction.pdf, accessed June 11, 2009.

"I have argued the importance of managers rec-
ognizing the potential that lies within everyone
they manage and of treating them accordingly.
It is, however, even more important for people to
recognize their own hidden potential."

Coaching can systematically reveal to individuals what
is currently hidden from them in their own hearts, but
why focus on just certain specific individuals, when
every person in the whole organization ideally needs
to also come on board? What is it realistically that all
workers desperately want from their jobs? Certainly
pay if they are not yet financially independent, but even
for those who are, work holds out a promise of much
more affirmation.

To get a further sense of the value of coaching for busi-
nesses, let us look at the International Coach Federa-
tion survey of 210 coaching clients. They were looking
for demographic data and feedback about the value of
coaching:

"70% believed business coaching is 'very
valuable.'" Some of the outcomes were:

- 62.4% smarter goal-setting

- 60.5% more balanced life

- 57.1% lower stress levels

- 52.4% more self-confidence

- 43.3% improvement in quality of life

- 25.7% more income

> Business coaching isn't just for people who have no grasp on what they are doing. It's effective for anyone who wants to better manage their professional and personal life. Even those who think they have everything under control can learn something. People don't just use business coaching to make more money as the statistics on business coaching show. They use it to improve the overall quality of their life.[44]

Without doubt then coaching has what it takes to make a difference and that quickly too. These results are typical of what is currently being realized by coaching across the globe.

---

44 Lyn Troyer, http://www.articlesbase.com/internet-articles/business-coaching-statistics-is-it-worthwhile-730433.html , accessed on June 12, 2009.

CHAPTER VII - THE GLOBAL LONGING

We are in the midst of a shrinking global village (Marshall McLuhan) with new challenges arising directly from the implications of that reality. Robert Rosen[45] explains it as follows:

> "Because globalization and technology have leveled the playing field, and since we've reached a high level of sophistication in our systems and processes, our people provide our only remaining competitive advantage. Companies such as Toyota, Vivendi, and Motorola understand this. They mobilize three key global assets: people, relationships, and culture. They work hard to develop cultures of "globally literate" leaders at all levels: leaders who develop their own potential and that of others, who cultivate collaborative relationships, and who manage their own culture and the cultures of others."

This is why companies are ripe for learning how to leverage the coaching communication skills for greater success. Rosen is still focusing on leaders, but by now I expect the dualistic yin and yang concept of leaders and followers has you realizing, both are equally in view here for obvious reasons. Every edge which can be gained ought to be, for every employee in the entire

---

45   Robert Rosen, *Global Literacies (New York, NY: Simon & Schuster, 2000).*

organization is valuable to the bottom line. In the past people were more tolerant of hierarchical organizations and being bossed around, than they now are. Today flatter organizational profiles are being introduced to address this and collaboration and team work among functional equals, is what many workers are coming to expect. This is no longer a merely wishful dream, but through coaching communication skills, can now materialize into reality. James Stanford[46] of Petro-Canada explains his company communication strategy as follows: "Maximizing business success requires personal and economic success for all–and we actively pursue this common goal. Today, there are sacred principles in the way we treat our employees, consistently applied across all parts of the organization." Note his emphasis on every employee. So who should apply these coaching principles? Better yet, who can afford not to apply them?

Coaching is exploding prolifically all across the globe. Books on coaching are also regularly being published now. Monthly news magazines and training facilities are also coming on line to equip coaches. Many nations have national coaching organizations already established and others are trying to link with their neighbors or within their regions. A number of these organizations are also attempting to become the global representative for coaching and the standard bearer of solid values and ethics. It is an exciting time for this new industry and many thousands of people are training as coaches, to bolster the numbers already practicing. Increasingly companies are

---

46   Robert Rosen, *Global Literacies* (New York, NY: Simon & Schuster, 2000).

seeing the benefit of gaining the coaching advantage and have begun to hire coaches, to help them change their paradigm. Conversely others are attempting to train their own leaders and managers as coaches to keep the process going permanently as an in-house project.

A book which I found useful and have not mentioned here yet is Hunt and Weintraub's, *The Coaching Organization*[47]. It contains practical advice about how to tangibly move an organization fully into the coaching model. It was well researched and makes a solid case for moving forward with coaching. Another way to implement coaching on either a personal or organizational level is to simply contract with a life coach and begin to derive the benefit. Any coach worthy of their title, will be able and excited to provide further information specifically tailored to your situation. Use the power of the internet and Google for a coach either in your area or, since most coaching in the US at least is done by phone, more importantly, suitable to your specific challenges, according to their advertising, regardless of their location. The US Army has the slogan "Be all that you can be; join the Army," but coaching will also make that empowerment possible. It is truly exciting to see the positive impact coaching can and is having in many places right now. I want to close this section with a great coaching summary from an article by Cook and Rosinki[48]:

47 *James Hunt and Joseph Weintraub, The Coaching Organization (Thousand Oaks, CA: Sage Publications, Inc., 2007).*

48 *Richard Cook & Philippe Rosinski, COACHING ACROSS CULTURES (http://myglobalcoach.com/_wsn/page10.html) accessed on June 13, 2009.*

"Coaching values well-being and fulfillment. It emphasizes self-care, quality of life, and human growth. Coaching is also a method to enhance performance and a leadership style that gets results. Coaches help people find practical solutions to the concrete challenges they face: how can people make the most of their time, improve leadership and communication, achieve ambitious work goals, have a better life balance, understand and use emotions, develop their creative thinking, overcome harmful stress, establish constructive relationships, and so on?"

This cogent statement on the role of coaching will move us nicely into the next subject of how we should communicate.

CHAPTER VIII - COMMUNICATING LIKE JESUS

Coaching is a neutral tool which can be used in a purely humanistic fashion, or as a tool God has placed in the hands of Bible believers. Believers who seek to honor God's work in people's lives find coaching is a great way in which to show them how He is working through the spiritual coaching process. One on one, a coach and coachee can make wonderful progress into understanding the workings of God within them. They may both become more aware of God's activity, simply through wise questions being appropriately asked by the coach. It is imperative to note a coach does not carry the solutions and answers, like a mentor or teacher. This is where the coach is communicating the most like Jesus did when He dealt with people on earth; He led them to make conclusions and decisions for themselves, simply through asking pertinent questions. It is also highly instructive to note that Jesus did not differentiate between believers and non-believers in implementing this approach. A coach understands and is skilled by practice in how to draw the coachee into a deeper place to make discoveries for themselves. Tony Stoltzfus explains it as follows:

> "Coaching is a faith discipline: if I have the faith to coach a person, I believe that I can take my hands off that individual's life and God will step in and do something incredible. Giving

responsibility to others instead of taking responsibility for them is a key to developing leaders."[49]

This avoids creating dependency upon a leader- the coach, by conversely empowering the coachee to lead for themselves. That makes it quite obvious how this ties directly into what I have been explaining about the dualistic tension between leadership and followership. Here we have leaders communicating in a way that empowers followers to take quantum steps toward growth and maturity, both on the job and as people; without the follower becoming beholden to the leader. Motivation becomes internalized as opposed to always being extrinsic. Likewise initiative and responsibility are personally embraced by followers as they begin to realize the power and freedom of personal choice and their individual impact.

While all coaching does not incorporate the spiritual dimension, it does follow a similar methodology or praxis and so applies equally to all people and is still strategically communicating like Jesus. Tony Stotlzfus further notes:

> "The more you help those you lead take responsibility for their own lives, the less work it is for you! Coaching cuts the cord of dependence and unleashes people. What really matters in organizational leadership is not what you know, but whether you can relate... Coach training is all about upgrading your conversational and relational skills." *Ibid.*

49 Tony Stoltzfus, *Leadership Coaching* (Virginia Beach, VA: Personal, 2005).

The Andersons eagerly agree: "Successful leaders are those who coach—and not try to control—others."[50] Clearly my emphasis through communicating like Jesus is on giving away power as a leader, to those who are following.

Not to belabor the subject, but this communication style of coaching is now a passion area of conviction for me. It came as an 'aha' insight into my quest for the essence of leadership. Crane puts it this way: "Leadership effectiveness is dramatically affected through asking for, responding to, and following up on feedback, and those are the essential steps of Transformational Coaching."[51] He continues in this fashion: "A manager's task is simple—to get the job done and grow his staff. Time and cost pressures limit the latter. Coaching is one process which accomplishes both." *Ibid*

Communicating like Jesus did- coaching, seems to answer a significant part of what the essence of a leader truly is. However, if communication is really meant to be that way why would we say it only applies to leaders? Does it then not become more obvious why tension exists between the roles of leaders and followers? Every person must surely take full responsibility to communicate appropriately for the best of all around them. If we can come to accept leadership and followership as inseparable functions, devoid of titles and rank, but filled with personal responsibility for everyone to take ownership and fulfill our roles, we will see authentic

50 Dianna & Merrill Anderson, *Coaching that Counts (Burlington, MA: Elsevier Butterworth-Heinemann, 2005).*

51 Thomas G. Crane, *The Heart of Coaching (San Diego, CA: FTA Press, 2007).*

followership and leadership beginning to flow more naturally. We will also hopefully see the yin and yang tension of dynamic dualism between leadership and followership, become less tense and more dynamic. Growing communication skills for all through coaching will surely speed up this growth process.

CHAPTER IX - POST MODERN CHALLENGES TO TRUTH

In the modern academic world, which has now for all practical purposes disposed of absolutes[52], what basis can prove adequate for outlining foundational principles for leadership and followership to transpire for the mutual edification of all involved? Are we, when following the direction of this present thesis, destined to just swap one tyranny- by the egotistical leader, for another- that of the egotistical follower? How do we hope to get to the bottom of the issue if we no longer believe there is anything to the concept of grounded reality? Post modernism has given us so much space to draw our own conclusions in spite of anyone and anything to the contrary, that we now should effectively just blunder ahead in our own reality regardless.

Well, my reality says that approach is hopelessly bankrupt of all common sense and defies logic. Generally accepted reality says we have been created as people, quite distinct by design from the animal kingdom in one fundamental way; we worship. All people do in one way or another. Anthropology clearly teaches that people, wherever they find themselves on this planet, are involved in some way with a belief system regarding our Maker and their need to please, or appease them. Since we are hard wired with this inalienable right to

52 http://www.thetruthproject.org/ accessed June 22, 2009.

respond to our own inner feelings by worship, why do we permit our intellect to be so plundered as to believe no communication from our Maker exists? Surely if a car manufacturer feels the need to supply a buyer with a manual to correctly operate and maintain that vehicle, we can at least expect the Creator of all we know, to be equally responsible and permit us a record of their intentions, so that we do not remain in the dark of ignorance. Why in the same vain then we would expect that being relational and interpersonal beings as we are, the Creator would be a merely impersonal force? That hardly seems a reasonable expectation. Were we created vastly superior to our source or merely a similar representation?

Cultural anthropology rapidly leads us to the insight that among almost all the cultural groups of this world, records exist of the ancient stories passed down from antiquity; explaining origins. As these have been codified and recorded in books, they have taken on the role of revelation; at least from our ancestors, but also possibly via them from the real deity. The concept of the Golden Rule would be the basic common denominator among them, with radical departure after that into myriad different contradictory explanations. So we cannot accept all equally as revelation from whatever Creator exists, but we do realize that human nature normally claims revelation as fundamental and centrally significant to living. Seemingly we could check the reliable authenticity of each manuscript from external and internal evidence and come to a satisfactory conclusion about which one would be most believable. The problem does not exist where they all agree as already mentioned, but this becomes necessary because of the aforesaid contradictory nature among them, logically requiring the discounting of the less reliable sources lacking that adequate vindication of value.

We then realize this has functionally already happened by the way people live today. Take the fact that by the personal choice of people, the largest global acceptance of any one such book is the runaway best seller the Bible. If God has spoken, a profound majority of people agree it is through the Bible and so when we read the Bible we take it objectively at face value, as believable revelation. Does it then prove true in our experience as well? Certainly, the same mysteriously supernatural experiences it declares, become subjectively part of our daily reality, confirming it to be at least a trust worthy book, but obviously also much more- the clear self disclosure of God as it claims.

The alternative option exists to disbelieve it at face value, but then one is left with only weaker alternative options and that is not a logical choice. What then does that 'most commonly accepted' revelation say about absolutes and truth? It would seem we have a solid basis among billions of people to see some fundamental rules and principles, by which to order this yin and yang of leadership followership. We do find that parameters have been set within the Bible by which we have freedom to explore the dimensions of this dynamic dualism, and we will next explore those when we add the gender dimension, in the specific context of Christian marriage.

I am setting the context this specifically while fully aware the debate goes on in the nation about what constitutes a marriage. I have intentionally done this to stick with what we accept as revelation and simplify the discussion accordingly. In other words a clear choice exists- believe God and stop the endless debate, He has clearly expressed the supposedly evasive answer already, or ignore God and carry on debating regard- less. Marriage offers a clearly troubled area where leadership questions around gender have raged for long among those who claim to believe the Bible. In this next section I will address those issues directly.

SECTION III - CHRISTIAN MARRIAGE

In this final section of exploring the dynamic dualism of the yin and yang of leadership followership, I have committed to using the Bible as revelation from our Maker to extrapolate the application of these concepts, to the Christian marriage relationship. This adds the issue of gender to all the discussions that have gone before in Sections I and II. With the workplace about evenly filled by both genders now, but leadership still predominantly male controlled, it is imperative that we understand the best available way to work in harmony. I want to steer a mature course through the many options open to viewing the gender challenges, based upon what I deduce from Scripture to be God's revealed perspective. In essence men and women are very different species of the same human race. Valued as equals by God and endowed with specific enablement and bias to fully accomplish His intent as male and female human beings.

Communication is always crucial and between two vastly different people along coaching lines of mutual respect and affirmation, should adequately negate their natural tendencies, which are usually all too prevalent when unbridled, but seldom helpful. This form of communication is designed to edify and encourage people to be their best. Men and women must be willing to compromise who they naturally are, to function responsibly with their gender opposites. This is not phony, or hypocritical, but strategically wise for the greatest affect. Few people view the term husband or wife, as a title or an office. Yet the fact remains leadership needs to take place and so does followership, or else the marriage relationship will go nowhere. Would it be helpful in this context to substitute the term leadership with initiator and that of follower with responder? That would mean we look at marriage as the yin and yang of initiating and responding. Then it would possibly be easier to see the point I am trying to make in this entire manuscript; that leaders are not the mega important persons in spite of all the others, we so commonly accept today. If appropriate response does not follow initiating, we will have a dynamic tension to deal with. In marriage that happens a lot of the time and with an unseen enemy seeking the destruction of God's purpose and intent for marriage, it is no small wonder marriage is such volatile territory.

In the Genesis account of creation, God made a man and then designed woman as an ideal helpmeet for him. He made them distinctly different both physically and psychologically, with a wonderful strategy in mind for these differences to serve His purposes. It is very helpful to accept the differences this way, rather than try to pretend they do not exist or fight for an equality that rarely exists. Men on average remain bigger, faster, and stronger and that is just reality. Anything requiring those assets will usually be better performed by a man. Together they were then called to serve God by obediently following His lead into being fruitful and multiplying, going forth and subduing the whole world. Here the general account is recorded in Genesis 1:

> "26Then God said, "Let Us make man in Our image, according to Our likeness; and let them rule over the fish of the sea and over the birds of the sky and over the cattle and over all the earth, and over every creeping thing that creeps on the earth." 27God created man in His own image, in the image of God He created him; male and female He created them. 28God blessed them; and God said to them, "Be fruitful and multiply, and fill the earth, and subdue it; and rule over the fish of the sea and over the birds of the sky

> and over every living thing that moves on the earth."[53]

Some initial concepts immediately arise from this general statement about the beginning. People were made equal in value, in spite of gender differences, since they were made in God's image. God was clear in His provision that one woman was enough to adequately be one man's life long accomplice. Equally, that she would quite naturally by design be his gender opposite. Having babies was part of God's intention for populating the planet and man was not designed to have them himself. Neither however was the woman able to have babies without the man. God designed so primary a function to only become possible by their symbiotic cooperation. Together they can achieve much, but alone they will not fulfill the creation purposes of God. Genesis says God that it was 'not good' for the man to be alone and that was why God gave him woman as his helper. Ruling over the earth was given as a command to them both as a human team to accomplish.

In Genesis 2 the account is repeated in more detail as to the process involved, as follows:

> "[7]Then the LORD God formed man of dust from the ground, and breathed into his nostrils the breath of life; and man became a living being. [8]The LORD God planted a garden toward the east, in Eden; and there He placed the man whom He had formed.

---

53 *Bible (Nashville, TN: Broadman, 1999).*

[18]Then the LORD God said, "It is not good for the man to be alone; I will make him a helper suitable for him."

[21]So the LORD God caused a deep sleep to fall upon the man, and he slept; then He took one of his ribs and closed up the flesh at that place. [22]The LORD God fashioned into a woman the rib which He had taken from the man, and brought her to the man. [23]The man said, "This is now bone of my bones, and flesh of my flesh; she shall be called Woman, because she was taken out of Man." [24]For this reason a man shall leave his father and his mother, and be joined to his wife; and they shall become one flesh."[54]

Here the detail shows the man came first and the woman was designed to match his needs; to best be able to blend with him as a helper. God clarified they were to be equals for they were made of the same substance and given the same general calling. God even spelled out His desire for the man to leave his parents when it was time to take a wife, and begin on his own from there. This way every new couple was a brand new start on the life journey of producing new offspring; who would eventually also make a new start themselves in due course. People would multiply and move ever outward from that local beginning to occupy the entire globe. Only the man is told to leave his parents because it was taken for granted his wife would already have left her family when he took her from them to marry him. It had to be spelled out to him and

54 Ibid.

his parents though; that just staying with them after marriage was not acceptable to God. Staying with his folks would not facilitate God's plan for people to fully occupy earth and it would never be realized.

A major dimension revealed in this passage has been lost by our generation and so most preachers even neglect to remind us that God revealed marriage occurred by two people becoming 'one flesh'. In other words when people have sexual intercourse God sees them as one flesh; married. Sex was therefore intended by God to be exclusively for marriage. God never intended 'multiple' partners, nor multiple marriages. Neither was sex ever considered dirty or exclusively for procreation. All these aberrations have been introduced by our neglecting the plain teaching of Scripture and we suffer loss accordingly. The prophet Malachi was used by God to remind us of both the purpose and duration of marriage in chapter 2:

> "[13]This is another thing you do: you cover the altar of the LORD with tears, with weeping and with groaning, because He no longer regards the offering or accepts it with favor from your hand. [14]"Yet you say, 'for what reason?' because the LORD has been a witness between your companion and your wife by covenant. [15]"But not one has done so who has a remnant of the Spirit and what did that one do while he was seeking a godly offspring? Take heed then to your spirit, and let no one deal treacherously against the wife of your youth. [16]"For I hate divorce," says the LORD, the God of Israel, "and him who covers his garment with wrong," says the LORD of

hosts. "So take heed to your spirit; that you do not deal treacherously.""[55]

What this generation battles to hear and accept is that this is our Maker declaring what will bring fulfillment and peace. Divorce and promiscuity are both pandemic and the media culture[56] promotes the view that sex is merely a recreational activity to be engaged in without negative repercussions. The explosion of STD's in just the past few decades is surely evidence alone of the ignorance of believing all will be alright, while flaunting what God has decreed. Yet, that God readily wants people to engage in sex and enjoy each other is quite apparent from reading 1 Corinthians 7:

> "[1]Now concerning the things about which you wrote, it is good for a man not to touch a woman. [2]But because of immoralities, each man is to have his own wife, and each woman is to have her own husband. [3]The husband must fulfill his duty to his wife, and likewise also the wife to her husband. [4]The wife does not have authority over her own body, but the husband does; and likewise also the husband does not have authority over his own body, but the wife does. [5]Stop depriving one another, except by agreement for a time, so that you may devote yourselves to prayer, and come together again so that Satan will not tempt you because of your lack of self-control."[57]

55 Ibid.
56 John G. West, Darwin Day in America, (Wilmington, DE: ISI Books, 2007).
57 Bible (Nashville, TN: Broadman, 1999).

The leading issue here is clearly that the appropriate relationships must be established prior to sexual engagement. The previous chapter had listed all the inappropriate sexual connections people were making to their own detriment. God intends sex to exclusively happen in marriage. Once marriage has taken place, each partner is to serve the needs of the other, to their mutual heart's content. This was clearly revealed by God because so much immorality was taking place with sex regularly happening outside of official marriage and often, too seldom within it. Both offenses are serious destroyers of the plan and intent of the Creator and Designer of life for warm passionate relationships of mutual joy and edification. God's plan provides a safe context for the vulnerability of sex to take place for the mutual edification of the married partners. It is also significant to note God emphasizes the equal nature between the partners by giving control of their own bodies to the other partner. No grounds therefore exist anymore for physical strength or gender idiosyncrasies- like women regularly 'having headaches' and being unavailable, to play a decisive role. By this I simply state the typical errors married couples get themselves into by the men usually demanding and trying to force sex and woman refusing claiming weaknesses of some description leaving them unavailable. Each gender tends more one way than the other; men revert to physical control and woman to emotional. These are merely statements of normal default settings typically found in each gender. Children would then also be raised and they would be secure within the solid home life provided by these faithful parents in their stable relationship. Ignoring this revealed strategy and context for sex, is leading to the serious erosion of the family unit, and inevitable destruction of society as we have known it for over two hundred years in the US.

Where did the problem set in that causes male chauvinism or the distasteful female backlash reaction known as feminism? To hear from God we need to return to Genesis 3- the passage is too long to quote here, so I will paraphrase what it says. The evil presence personified on earth as Satan or the devil, appeared to the woman, because the man was not paying attention and seduced her into disobeying God's command to not eat of the Tree of the Knowledge of Good and Evil. She not only ate and immediately fell from the state of innocence into the state of sinfulness, but shared the fruit with her husband and he too fell into sinfulness. She was deceived and disobedient, while he was merely absent and disobedient. It is instructive to hear God's assessment of the future between them. He addressed the woman as follows in Genesis 3:

> " [16]To the woman He said, "I will greatly multiply your pain in childbirth, in pain you will bring forth children; yet your desire will be for your husband, and he will rule over you."[58]

The little word 'desire' may cause some confusion. The same word is used in the next chapter (4:7) where God warned Cain about sin crouching at the door and its 'desire' was for him. It is not a word about 'lust', but about control. From this we see a warning from God that a natural tendency in wives will be the attempt to control their husbands. Many husbands do not

58 *Ibid.*

see this as a problem, but like Adam, are scarce when they should be on duty. That is not what God intends; rather He clearly states to the wife: 'he will rule over you'. Please note these are not generic expectations of interaction between men and women, but exclusively between a man and his wife. However, it is important to establish these gender differences in tendency and call, by God's revelation, so that we can appropriately apply the leadership followership principles already established.

Next God addressed the man as follows:

> "[17]Then to Adam He said, "Because you have listened to the voice of your wife, and have eaten from the tree about which I commanded you, saying, 'You shall not eat from it'; cursed is the ground because of you; in toil you will eat of it all the days of your life."[59]

Does God still have a problem with the man listening to his wife; because many wives testify that they have a problem because they simply won't? Again, the context merely determines that God did not want the man to be led by the wife while she was deceived. He as the 'head' has to determine, we will see this dimension shortly, if her input is valid and sober. God does not want him to just politely obey and follow her lead regardless. We could hardly apply coaching principles to marriage if the man is never intended to listen to his wife; but mercifully that is not the case. This concept is repeated in teaching revealed in Ephesians 5:

59   *Ibid.*

"22Wives, be subject to your own husbands, as to the Lord. 23For the husband is the head of the wife, as Christ also is the head of the church, He Himself being the Savior of the body. 24But as the church is subject to Christ, so also the wives ought to be to their husbands in everything."

As head of the wife in the marriage relationship we have the intent of God that the man should be to his wife just like Christ is to the church. Earlier, I showed how the modern church has functionally lost this idea of Christ as anything other than the figure head leader. Many marriages have tragically suffered similarly. Our lack of a healthy church to look at and see what husbands should be doing, is still no excuse for not doing it. Husbands need to understand this headship is not a dominant role, but on the contrary; that of a servant. We are called to love our wives as Christ loves the church and He gave His very life for the church to come into existence. According to Bruce Wilkinson[60] this concept of headship has two main features: for the husband to "stand before" his wife in protection and provision. The husband must provide for the wife and protect her total well being. This clearly ties in with the failure of Adam back in the garden when the devil was able to seduce her in his absence from this role. We see a clear elaboration of the provision dimension in what God reveals in 1Timothy 5: "8But if anyone does not provide for his own, and especially for those of his household, he has denied the faith and is worse than an unbeliever." Sober words in a day when so many husbands fail to

---

60 Bruce Wilkinson, *A Biblical Portrait of Marriage* (Atlanta, GA: Walk Thru the Bible, 2008).

provide, but expect their wife to do at least half. We will see in due course how this can be effectively worked through in relationship, but seek here to only establish duty, as revealed by God.

As a licensed marriage officer I have been required to do plenty of pre-marital and marital counseling with marriage partners. In these fruitful environments for problem solving, it amazed me how people have evolved God's requirements by twisting and misconstruing. Husbands seem to vary between the owner/boss/lord perspective, of those who seek to control and 'parent' their spouse on the one hand, or the doormat husband on the other, who has long since given up hope of ever being allowed to be a man around his controlling wife. Wives in general of course tend to be more willing to accept the husband as the protector and provider, but usually would still like the last word on things. The whole idea of submission by wives to their husbands has fallen on hard times in the culture where feminism is as dominant as it currently is in the western world. However, if understood correctly, submission is placing oneself by choice within the realm God intends for happiness as a wife. That takes at least as much faith as the man needs to fulfill his twin roles as the head. Seen as the way God has revealed things to be ordered, changes the discussion entirely between spouses from one of superior and inferior, to one of choosing to obey God or not. If God's revelation is rejected at this point, the application of the principles will be harder to implement. God requires the husband to protect and provide as he loves his wife in obedience to God. The wife obeys God by respecting her husband and choosing to subject herself to him in all things. Only one can be taking the ultimate responsibility and God says that will be the man. It is not about who feels this is right, or about who is superior. It is simply what God has chosen and revealed. The man's tendency will be to abdicate and the woman's tendency will be to take control. Now let us look more intently at gender implications in general. As I have shown these passages reflect God's heart for a man and his own wife. I want to take the essence of what has been seen as female and the essence of what is male and look at how those gender differences lead to tension, or effectivity in the workplace.

In the New Testament book of Galatians, God makes a clear case for the benefits of the Gospel in every person's life. Galatians 3: "²⁸There is neither Jew nor Greek, there is neither slave nor free man, there is neither male nor female; for you are all one in Christ Jesus." Whether or not one has personally responded to God by faith in Jesus, these concepts have already been brought into reality by the work of Christ on the cross of Calvary. This revelation shows that by the shed blood of Christ, the sinful practice of people to elevate men as superior and denigrate women as inferior; has been destroyed. God sees no difference between the value of men or women. Jesus certainly modeled that by the way He related to both men and women during His lifetime. The application of that truth is then that we may never call into question the value of employees based on gender criteria. This can however be a delicate issue to implement fairly.

When I worked in a national bank as a young man, we were under an equal pay for equal work jurisdiction and that was applied to mean the same pay package for men and women of similar rank. However, what was fundamentally unfair in that policy was the monthly provision of five extra 'sick days' for women with full pay, to deal with their cycle requirements if necessary. Surely common sense would accept that was then no longer equal work and so could not equate to equal pay? By all means offer those in need of this exemption the full benefit, but do not pay them for the days they take in exercise of their right. That way, those still working without the right and those working without exercising their right, were doing equal work and entitled to equal pay. This covers the equality dimension, but what about diversity?

Traditionally men worked the farm and women kept the house and little children. Naturally that tended toward boys joining their dads as they grew doing farm chores and girls helping their mom's do the household chores. A natural division of labor existed without overt rules about gender tasks. When school came along it was natural for single adult ladies to teach the younger children and older women to teach the girls and men to teach the older boys. Nurses were women and men became doctors. Those simple applications from an earlier agricultural society here in the US no longer fit reality and so radical changes have come about. What must also be closely noted is that other agricultural societies did not necessarily follow this western model. In much of Africa for instance the women are involved in the managing of all the life processes, like cultivating crops, collecting firewood, tending the livestock, preparing food and making the beer and having the babies. Men were the warriors who hunted for the family table, won new lands and protected the tribe. Young boys learned the skills needed for warfare while tending cattle. It was still clearly a division of labor along gender lines, but not the same lines as in the West. Today those lines have become increasingly blurred as education has opened new career possibilities globally for both.

Today men are not only becoming nurses as they desire, but women are able to become medical doctors and practice as they desire. Even the US armed forces are increasingly opening up to a largely gender free experience. Education has also become thoroughly integrated with men or women teaching any age or gender student, across the entire spectrum. So organizations today are necessarily also largely gender free. What have been slower to open up are top executive positions for women, yet new glass ceilings are being shattered ever more constantly. Is this an acknowledgement that differences no longer exist between the genders?

Generalizations are always dangerous so need to be made with great care to be considered seriously. It would be a great loss to all if the beauty of our gender diversity were permitted to be lost in exchange for sameness. It is definitely not the same for a student to have a same, as opposed to opposite gender professor. Neither is the style of that professor devoid of their gender influence. In my recent past taking doctoral levels classes alternatively from male and female professors, certain characteristics were plainly visible. Nurturing, encouragement and a gentle listening ear were certainly characteristic of one gender group over the other. Conversely, blunt directness, aggression and harshness could be lumped on the other gender, as defining of those professors. Were I but able to survey you now as my readers, I wonder how many need an explanation of which gender I was referring to respectively? I am not giving one because I am convinced those differences are really still that apparent to all of us. Please note nothing of relative intelligence or professional expertise was mentioned, as in any way relevant. So it appears gender diversity falls more naturally into the style category, than competence.

Many people seeking counsel for marital discomforts came to me with a similar question regarding duties within the marriage. Not the obvious duties like breast feeding babies which only women are equipped to perform; but debatable questions like who should handle the finances for example. If the husband's role is to provide, then the assumption follows that surely he is the one who must balance the check book and pay the bills. But in reality no such rule exists anywhere. God certainly has not spoken on the matter that I have been able to find so far. When God delivered the wife as the helpmeet to the husband and she has superior book keeping skills, she would be a huge help to her husband by doing the books. She would be fulfilling a primary condition of her role very well. The husband by definition must provide, but there is no similarly clear definition about who must pay the bills or how. May the wife also be employed outside the home and in that manner bring in extra income? Again, would that be her fulfilling her God given role to be a helpmeet to her husband? If so, she should definitely do it. What about a wife with a vastly better paying career than her husband- friends of ours in Texas were like this: he was a carpenter on a construction crew and she had a PhD in Math and worked for Bell Helicopter Company on the development team of the Osprey. God has built the flexibility into the Christian marriage relationship that the definition of the wife being the helpmeet covers a multitude of these situation conclusions. Certainly only the wife can carry and deliver babies and experiences lactation, but beyond that everything else seems to be pretty open to their working out who does what and when. Wives will generally speaking be the stronger nurturing partner and tender hearted toward the millions of issues little children focus all their attention on. Husbands will equally generally be harder on their children, pushing for rapid progress and achievement. Men seem to be harder wired for competition and winning, while women want to include everybody and gravitate toward everyone feeling good, with nobody excluded. Personal discipline does not however appear to be a gender consistent given.

Bruce Wilkinson[61] again says that a wife according to Scripture is called the "despot of the oikos." This is like the queen of the castle. The home is her domain to make the nest the way she chooses and a wise husband will give her all the space and latitude she needs. Her sense of well being rests upon being able to express herself appropriately in her living space. This is no patronizing position either; the Proverbs 31 wife is an amazingly resourceful and productive person:

> "[10]An excellent wife, who can find? For her worth is far above jewels. [11]The heart of her husband trusts in her, and he will have no lack of gain. [12]She does him good and not evil all the days of her life. [13]She looks for wool and flax and works

61 Bruce Wilkinson, A Biblical Portrait of Marriage, (Atlanta, G.A. Walk Thru the Bible. 2008).

with her hands in delight. [14]She is like merchant ships; she brings her food from afar. [15]She rises also while it is still night and gives food to her household and portions to her maidens. [16]She considers a field and buys it; from her earnings she plants a vineyard. [17]She girds herself with strength and makes her arms strong. [18]She senses that her gain is good; her lamp does not go out at night. [19]She stretches out her hands to the distaff, and her hands grasp the spindle. [20]She extends her hand to the poor, and she stretches out her hands to the needy. [21]She is not afraid of the snow for her household, for all her household are clothed with scarlet. [22]She makes coverings for herself; her clothing is fine linen and purple. [24]She makes linen garments and sells them, and supplies belts to the tradesmen. [25]Strength and dignity are her clothing, and she smiles at the future. [26]She opens her mouth in wisdom, and the teaching of kindness is on her tongue. [27]She looks well to the ways of her household, and does not eat the bread of idleness. [28]Her children rise up and bless her; her husband also, and he praises her, saying: [29]"Many daughters have done nobly, but you excel them all."

This passage clearly shows the rich diversity this wife participated in from within her castle. God has never been opposed to women in the workforce, not even to wives being there. What has caused damage though is neglect of the home functions by wives seeking to be professionals in the market place, as their main avenue to find significance. It is a sad indictment upon husbands when their wives are so unfulfilled in their function at home, they go out seeking fulfillment in secondary places. Of course part of the blame also rests solidly on those wives themselves for failing to discover their primary role in life and find the God intended, deep and lasting satisfaction through it.

Husbands must focus on the twin duties of protection and provision for their wives and families. They have latitude to do whatever is legal and advantageous to accomplish the aforementioned goals. Wives need to be loved and feel it; nothing on earth does this better than the security of provision for and protection of them, by their husband. Husbands need to be resourceful to communicate love through practical channels as well as purely romantic emotional ones too. People are multifaceted as physical, spiritual and soulish beings. The Christian marriage is the avenue for all of these to be most fully expressed and realized with another human being God has offered us on earth. God purposefully placed two opposite people in the context of love in Christian marriage for His purposes to be fulfilled on earth. We embrace or ignore that to our own personal gain or peril. For that simple reason let me take us back to the dynamic tension of the yin and yang of leadership.

Gender issues afford us rich diversity in our organizations, but are potentially fraught with pitfalls. No boss can wisely ignore gender differences without losing a major part of the team. Yet neither can any boss so elevate gender differences they are seen to be sexist by discriminating accordingly. The desire of leaders must be to encourage followers to follow and a sensitive approach must be engaged to navigate these waters calmly. There is an appropriate way to relate to women and men as employees, how that is of course depending on whether you as the boss are either a woman or a man. Multiple challenges exist. That is why I tried to demonstrate the subtle differences in practical ways within the gender issues of marriage. I never dealt with marital infidelity, but that comes up in the workplace constantly. Do you flirt with or entertain flirting from your employees? That too is a minefield in the gender issue discussion. Let us move on that note to communication in marriage, as an illustration of the issues to be noted in business communication too.

CHAPTER XII - COMMUNICATION

When opposites communicate it is potentially grist for the comedian mills. Ask any two married people and you will quickly find one is fast, while one is slow; one is punctual while the other does not have a clue or concern about time. One will be talkative while the other the silent type. One will be loud while the other will be soft spoken. One will have cold feet and the other not even know what that means. Of course one will feel the heat and the other will feel the cold. One will rise early while the other will stay up late. One will see minute detail and be picky, while the other is into the big picture and doesn't sweat the minutia and that is just the tip of the proverbial marital iceberg. It is the need screaming out for healthy communication, because without it the marriage will inevitably be doomed. If our ancestors in the garden got into trouble through an interfering enemy seeking to destroy them, as we read above, what makes us think that enemy has left, or will leave God's intention for marriage alone, to work out nicely? That is not going to happen and only good communication will be able to protect God's interests in things working out as He desires.

I wish to bring the concept of coaching into the discussion at this point. If a husband and wife can learn to apply the coaching communication principle of deferring to the other, they will have a much greater chance for marital success. By deferring, I mean coaches listen carefully to the other, and in marriage this is an essential requirement for communication to take place well. Coaches do not offer opinions and suggestions, rather they will ask questions to explore further meaning and ensure they are grasping accurately what is being said. Obviously they also uncover yet unspoken issues to also work through; which of course, the coachee is willing to do. If spouses can do this for each other, in spite of their mega differences, they will fully communicate both the respect and the love, each specifically needs. This will not be a formal structured coaching type relationship with appointments and fees for a specific duration. Rather it will become the ongoing way in which two people in love, honor each other by both listening and questioning in a two way coaching style of communicating. That way both partners will grow and constantly challenge the other positively to also do so. This is a very intentional and responsible way to deal with the serious commitment one makes in getting married.

The marriage vows used for making that commitment for instance are made to God, since marriage is entirely His idea. Can you imagine that some guy came up with this? Watching sport on TV in a pub, one man suddenly grabs the remote and mutes the show. "Guess what?" he announces. "I have just decided to give up all my conquests and forsaking my freedom, I will commit myself in marriage to just one woman for the rest of my life." How many guys would cheer that idea? Sound in any way plausible? No way. God is the author of the marriage idea and it is a sacrificial decision for everyone who participates in it to make and then faithfully keep. Of course people can and do get married in places other than church buildings, but they nevertheless stand to do so, whether or not they are aware, before their Creator and not just each other, in front of their witnesses. It is inadequate to exchange vows merely between each other, as that defeats the major purpose of a Christian wedding. Invoking the Father's pleasure in one's marriage is a very wise and yet sobering thing to undertake. It is committing oneself to perform the marriage according to His revelation and intent for marriage, as we have seen above. This is not bad news at all, because special grace from Him follows any commitment to do things the way He reveals. Can any married person today say they have all that it takes to be successful in marriage and some added grace would not be needed and welcomed?

I bought a house in Tennessee from a couple once. They had lived together for thirteen years without legally marrying; because his father refused to approve their marriage. However, when the father died they went ahead and got married. Well I bought the house two years later when they divorced. How does that make sense you ask? They lived together in sin, for thirteen years, but could not make two years succeed when done God's way? Again I say it is God's idea to marry and the devil's idea to live in sin. So who do you think hassles married people: someone far more sinister and deadly than any mother in law? Don't get involved in something God planned and intends, unless you have God's means to experience grace and then do it properly. Coaching will help everybody improve communication, but ultimately marriage in fellowship with God through Jesus Christ is the complete intention. So much so in fact, that the Father uses a marriage metaphor to reveal the church of Jesus Christ is His bride and headed toward the Marriage Feast of the Lamb. Communication in marriage is only full and complete when God Himself is personally included in the couple's communications. The yin and yang of the leadership followership dynamic will next be seen as the coaching communication style is applied to leadership issues within the Christian marriage.

CHAPTER XIII - LEADERSHIP

Nothing I have discussed so far about Christian marriage has had even a hint of leadership attached to it. I have studiously avoided the leadership followership dynamic until now. In the previous chapters as we looked at gender issues and then communication, I was highlighting the differences God has creatively included into the relational mix to keep things fresh and challenging. Having given a threefold task to married couples as we saw previously, it is now important to understand how leadership followership ideally works in marriage. If we can clearly see it working effectively here in a potentially fragile cross-gender relationship, we will hopefully grasp the potential for it working in less complex situations; like the workplace.

My premise remains that leadership is not based in essence on title or office, but flows functionally according to gifting and conviction in context. In marriage we have no title or office so we can ideally see how the yin and yang of leadership followership plays out. Take for example a very basic level of relationship between married partners and simply ask "Who leads in initiation of sexual intimacy?" Is it categorically possible to make a definitive statement which will always hold water for this one, or even often? I choose this topic because it is the precursor to many other potential developments in the relationship. My informed contention is that while men are traditionally seen as the hunters, many women today equally enjoy the role without violating anything stated by God. Both partners are responsible to be sensitive and responsive toward any lead the other takes to advance sexual intimacy. So leadership at this crucial point is not gender based. Neither then by definition is followership gender based either. Does a leadership statement of desire like "I want sex" sound like, even considerate, let alone loving, foreplay? No, leadership of that nature is unhelpful and will rarely evoke desired followership. If however, either spouse is feeling arousal they can freely lead the activity further and the other spouse is invited by God to respond positively by following their lead. This perfectly complies with my definition of leadership as appropriate function in context. I have counseled frustrated men and many equally frustrated women, because this does not always take place. Selfishness instead of generosity is all too often the followership response in marriage, to sexual advances from their spouse. That turnoff harms more than just their sex life. Begrudging compliance in followership does very little to better empower healthy engagement. Here the power of the follower is brutal, especially when they refuse to respond positively to the leadership initiative. Sex is therefore rated as one of the top three reasons for conflict in marriage. It is so fundamental to violating stated marriage commitments I find it hard to not see it as the major issue. If a person can be selfish toward a spouse's advances and willfully shun their expressed needs in preference to their own selfish desires, how much sacrificial love is being displayed? Not much at all. Well if love in marriage is selfish and self serving, how can it actually be deemed love at all? But enough of leadership and followership in the realm of sexual issues, if we think the point is well established that it is not gender based; let us now advance by agreeing the couple is having a baby.

Since both partners have been working, lifestyle expenses have grown to meet that income and now it is very hard to consider cutting back when there will be added expenses of a baby. However, this mother agrees to put her career on hold at least until the babies are all in school. That could equally be a leadership stance she felt entirely for herself, or followership to a specific request from the husband; either against or in agreement with her personal inner desires. This is my point about leadership and followership functioning in context without titles or offices. Neither spouse is the official boss and nor is either spouse the official employee. We have seen the husband's role as head is to love by providing and protecting and the wife is to respect him and function as his helpmeet. Both are equal partners, with leadership followership duties in the realm of totally equal responsibility to be mutually worked out as the need determines them to function.

Problems rarely arise when agreement reigns. It is when disagreement raises its head and a compromise solution is needed that two humble people must serve each other in mutual love, without being selfish, and trust that an agreement can be mutually reached. At work the next day, wearing whatever title they may carry, is it not highly likely these spouses will look more sensitively at their employees as people with feelings and choices to express? My contention is that if we can see these marriage relationships through to a higher level of mutual satisfaction, both partners will go to work empowering those around them with their new found victory in communication and we all win; as will the bottom line. Can it be said the couple obeyed their call to multiply when they have only one child? That is only replacing one of them; so no- that is diminishing, not multiplying. Until they get to number three, they are not being obedient. That is sufficient to illustrate leadership followership dynamic tensions in being fruitful and multiplying, next we will see them applied to 'filling the earth and subduing it'.

Looking at the intent of God that people occupy and dwell throughout the entire earth, we must feel quite a bit of satisfaction that we have at least accomplished that part of the plan. For the most part the entire earth is now occupied. Certainly the Chinese and Indians have excelled beyond all others in this department, but we have collectively met God's desire. Now the question arises are new marriages therefore exempt from the age old pattern God established to achieve His goal? I would think not, for one simple reason; every generation must obey God for themselves. Nobody can rest on the past accomplishments to avoid present obedience. Besides the call to go into all the earth to rule, remains a healthy approach for everyone to avoid becoming stale and ingrown. Since we effectively live in a global village now and everyone can pretty much enjoy comforts from home wherever they choose to settle, it is no longer the huge challenge it formerly was. Now to look at leadership followership challenges specifically, that faces a married couple seeking to be Christian in their lives as they go into the world.

Looking at the world, we quickly get the impression men have always been in the fore front of history and progress. Equally they have been the pirates, mass murderers, evil dictators and both the causes and solvers of world wars. Beyond the admission of historical reality however, did God have any specific input into the primacy of male leadership? Certainly if one looks at who was available to choose from, God had an equal opportunity to select women as He did to select men and yet He usually chose men. Occasionally of course He chose women completely against the normal flow of events and they did at least as well. Deborah[62] an Old Testament warrior leader is an example of this unexpected leadership role. However, the preponderance of evidence has women performing the domestic tasks they are more traditionally equipped to handle. Does that then set any precedent for the man to be expected to automatically be the leader in a marriage, with the wife equally automatically the follower? Culture may raise its demands at this point, but I am more concerned about dealing with the absolutes of God's revealed word. I cautiously challenge that we cannot find a deal breaking demand from God to this end, or even any strong suggestions. We must be very cautious to avoid making our cultural or even historical norms, equal to Scripture as authority in our lives. Cultures differ vastly but Scripture provides a universal norm for all. What we then accept, is that this strategy I am proposing has legitimacy for married couples to explore leadership followership within their own context and see how they can use the gift package of skills and convictions they have received, to move forward the

62 *Judges 4:4-14.*

most smartly. Man has tendencies just like the woman does, but they differ quite significantly as we saw earlier. If the man is quintessentially the warrior, prepared to conquer so that he can provide and protect, then the woman is equally the nurturer who will support and embrace with respect and encouragement. Take these roles and filter them through their individual abilities to come up with the functioning style of the specific married couple before you.

It would seem the man will be full of the ideas to go and explore and conquer, while the woman will be happy to participate and encourage; as long as she can avoid seeing the blood. My wife was delighted when our son decided to play gridiron football and listened excitedly to his stories of the workouts and preparation for the game. Well, attending the game in full support only lasted about ten minutes before she was a bundled of tears. "Why do boys like hurting each other?" she wanted to know. Deciding this kind of football was barbarian, her desire to encourage was overruled by her desire to protect and care, and she never attended another game. When I asked my son who had successfully played numerous other sports, what was best about football, he replied the legal right to hit people; "really smash them." He is a warrior and destined to conquer territories as he fulfills his destiny. But God will temper the impact of that drive by adding a help-meet who is wired very differently. Together they will need to find a balance as they go into the world. His natural tendencies will be balanced by hers and vice versa; together the fruit of their symbiotic relationship will be what we see. Who will lead and who will follow?

Surely by now it is apparent that is the wrong question. They will both lead and both follow, if it is to work successfully at all. They are equal before God and equally responsible to make it work. Context will determine whose gifts will emerge functioning as the leader in each specific incident and the other would be wise to follow accordingly. His tendencies will be present and so will hers, but their love and respect will empower communication and action accordingly. Will they stay in their present country or move to the other side of the world? Who knows, but they will be in agreement and excited whether they go or stay.

CONCLUSION

I have sought to present a fairly simple model for understanding leadership and followership in a more beneficial way than is typically practiced today. The old paradigm is spent and no longer works in our post modern world. Nobody enjoys feelings of inferiority and a system which creates losers and failures by definition, is doomed to failure. Why are followers condemned simply because they are not the hierarchical boss leader type, or even want to be? Social Darwinianism as a leadership model is spent and must go. People desire inclusion and acknowledgment more than ever before. More than that they actually want respect for their contribution and a sense that it is worthwhile to the organization.

Leadership according to my contribution is a function, manifest in context by gifting and insight. Leadership and followership are in a dualistic tension which I have referred to as the yin and yang of leadership follower-ship. These equally vital polar opposites are necessary for anything to get done, but they do not depend on title or office to exist. Followership is arrived at best by ac-cepting that following is the most basic call of God on all people. If we accept His invitation to follow Jesus and believe the Bible as His revealed Self disclosure, we become grounded in terms of values and commitments, which will enable faithful lives. As employees, these followers should be exemplary because they serve the One they are committed to and whatever organization employs them, will be better off for their presence and production; at a way higher level than before. Anyone grounded in a similar way with a commitment to a central non-negotiable Person or value, will potentially be equally excellent. This basic primary willingness to follow with courage and passion sets these workers apart from others for excellence. As they follow, they ironically lead by example and functionally lead whenever their gifting empowers them to do so. An organization which makes allowance for these employees will blossom. How do these followers communicate?

I presented the methodology of coaching communication as the supreme way we currently have available for people in any organization to all communicate. Of course coaching is way bigger than just the communication style it uses and I did not mean to diminish it in any way by not elaborating further about it as a marvelous tool in other ways as well. For my purposes here I chose to maintain that narrow emphasis. Coaching does not inform or disclose, rather it questions respectfully, leading to understanding on behalf of both participants. It empowers people rather than creating dependents. Improved self respect leads to confidence and improved delivery. It also leads to treating others the same way and they too will likewise be empowered. Finally I also included a discussion on gender issues, as it pertains to the yin and yang dynamic dualism of leadership followership by looking at Christian marriage.

Husbands in Christian marriages do not necessarily lead the couple in as many ways as often assumed.

Sure the general direction would be set by him, by virtue of the way God has wired him and his inner inclinations. However, God has called the couple to equality, but also specific roles and therefore leadership and followership emerge from both. So it is far more realistic to see leadership residing in the couple equally, rather than either one individually. As they implement coaching communication to defer to each other with love and respect, they will both be edified and grow into all they were intended to. Children added to their number will be trained by the model of their parent's how to do it themselves. Now what about implementing this in organizations?

Model Illustration:

Context determines function:

Switch in function employed:

Leadership - 'Initiative'   Followership- 'Response'

Figure 1   Figure 2

I am convinced this model is a foundational model for any people in business or personal relationships, to effectively manage the yin and yang tension of leadership followership. When we feel lifted and empowered by a relationship we value and cultivate it. Understanding that neither gender is either superior or inferior and then communicating with everyone in an affirming way will boost morale. Even when hierarchy still exists; with the usual titles and offices for the haves, effectively rendering the rest as have-nots, we will be making progress. When work is divided into functions and the best people are in the most appropriate places; doing what fulfils them, we will be making greater progress. This is demonstrated in figure 1 and 2 above. Both leadership and followership enabled to emerge according to need and gifting in the functional requirements of each situation.

WORKS CITED

Allan Metcalf. "American Dialect Society." *Americandialect.org*, January 6,, 2006. http://www.americandialect.org/Words_of_the_Year_2005.pdf. (accessed February 17, 2009).

Bible. Nashville: Broadman, 1999.

Bruce E. Winston. *Be A Leader For God's Sake*. Virginia Beach: School of Leadership Studies, 2002.

Calvin Miller, *The Empowered Leader*. (Nashville, T.N.: Broadman & Holman Publishers, 1995).

Charles Handy. *The Age of Paradox*. Boston: Harvard Business School Press, 1995.

Chip R. Bell. *Managers as Mentors: Building Partnerships for Learning*. San Francisco: Berrett-Koehler Publishers, Inc, 2002.

Christopher P. Neck, Tedd L. Mitchell, Charles C. Manz, Emmet C. Thompson II. *Fit To Lead*. (New York, N.Y.: St Martin's Press, 2004).

Daniel Harkavy. *Becoming a Coaching Leader*. Nashville, TN: Thomas Nelson, Inc, 2007.

Daniel Goleman. *Working with Emotional Intelligence*. New York: Bantam Books, 1998.

Daniel Goleman, Richard Boyatzis, Annie McKee. *Primal Leadership*. Boston, Massachusetts: Harvard School Press, 2002.

Del Tackett, *The Truth Project*, (Colorado Springs, CO: Focus on the Family, 2004).

Diane Ravitch. "Diane Ravitch Quotes." *Quotes.net. Stands4 Llc.* http://www.quotes.net/quote/16866/ (accessed March 28, 2009).

Dianna & Merrill Anderson. *Coaching that Counts.* Burlington, MA: Elsevier Butterworth-Heinemann, 2005.

Frank Viola & George Barna, *Pagan Christianity,* (Carol Stream, IL: Tyndale House Publishers Inc, 2008).

Gary Hamel, *Leading the Revolution* (Boston M.A.: Harvard Business School Press, 2000).

J. S. Nolan, *Followership Greater Than or Equal to Leadership.* (Education, 104(3), 311-312. 1984).

John G. West, *Darwin Day In America: How Our Politics and Culture Have Been Dehumanized in the Name of Science,* (Wilmington, DE: ISI Books, 2007).

Joseph Claburn. "Flexibility: today's leaders adjust, adapt, overcome." *Infantry Magazine* (March-April 2004): . www, http://findarticles.com/p/articles/mi_m0IAV/is_2_93/ai_n6124006/ (accessed March 28, 2009).

Leon Degrelle, The Enigma of Hitler, (*The Journal for Historical Review,* Volume 14 number 3, May/June 1994).

Marilyn Lustgarten. ""humility - A Leadership Imperative."" *Ezine @rticles*, April 7, 2008. http://ezinearticles.com/?Humility—A-Leadership-Imperative&id=1094341/ (accessed March 28, 2009).

Merriam-Webster. Review of *The Colbert Report*, by Stone Phillips. Stephen Colbert, ColbertNation.com. October 17, 2005.

Michael J Marquardt & Nancy O. Berger. *Global Leadership for the Twentieth Century*. New York: State University of New York Press, 2000.

Nelson Mandela, *Long Walk to Freedom,* (London,: Abacus, 1994).

Nicolo Machiavelli. *The Prince.* : , 1505.

Paul Hersey, *The Situational Leader* (Escondido, CA: Center for Leadership Studies, Inc. 1984, 2004).

Ricardo Semler, *The Seven Day Weekend*, (New York, N.Y.: Portfolio, 2004).

Robert K. Greenleaf, *Servant Leadership* (Mahwah, New Jersey: Paulist Press, 1977).

Robert Palestini, *A Path To Leadership The Heroic Follower*, (Rowman & Littlefield Education, Lanham, M.A.:2006).

Sue Mackey & Laura Tonkin. *Living Well, Working Smart*. Bothwell, WA: The Mackey Group Publishers Network, 2005.

Susan Smith Kuczmarski, Thomas D. Kuczmarski, *Values Based Leadership*. (Paramus, N.J.: Prentice-Hall Inc., 1995).

Sviatoslav Steve Seteroff, *Beyond Leadership to Followership*, (Victoria, B.C.: Trafford Publishing, 2003).

Thomas G. Crane. *The Heart of Coaching*. San Diego, CA: FTA Press, 2007.

Tony Stoltzfus. *Leadership Coaching*. Virginia Beach: Personal, 2005.